Odd Woman Out

EXPOSURE IN ESSAYS AND STORIES

Melanie Chartoff

This is a work of creative nonfiction.
In many cases, names, dates, and details have been changed to protect
the privacy of friends and family.

First Edition
Paperback ISBN 978-1-7352689-2-7
E-Book ISBN 978-1-7352689-3-4
Audiobook ISBN 978-1-7352689-4-1
Library of Congress Control Number 2020915830

Cover layout and typesetting: Stewart A. Williams

To my mother, who taught me
it's never too late to learn to love.

CONTENTS

INDECENT SEXPOSURE

Lying back on the table, I assume the position. Heels in stirrups, I expose my privates to an air-conditioned breeze. Time crawls by. Wish they'd let me read magazines in the lobby where the light's more flattering, where I wouldn't be alone with all these thoughts, obsessively writing them in my head, trying to find something funny in them to change my mood .

My ten-year try at forever love had turned loveless two years before. I'd rushed into a frantic romance, which ended when the guy recognized it as a rebound. This was followed by the realization that my last period had put the period on my menses, and probably put the period on men, period. Menopause? More like men-o-stop. And apparently my allotment of orgasms had expired with my eggs.

I look down on my body, depressed by the sight of my mammaries, full of memories that never knew milk. They look pretty good at half a century old, but of what interest are they now, except to doctors for poking and predicting?

I'd held onto my virginity until it was a twenty-two-year-old antique, a relic of my parents' prudery and my fear of losing control. In provincial New Haven in the sixties, going all the way had ruined many a girl's reputation. I was terrified of the treachery between boys' lips and legs and the mystery between my own. But in the early seventies, the Zeitgeists of Free Love and Liberation made being wholesome, virtuous, and moral look frigid, uptight, and screwed up. My holdover hymen was a curse. I had to get rid of it before my pull date. Nobody who knew my secret wanted to touch me. I seemed way too complicated. So, I got on the contraceptive Pill and made a magician I was assisting make my maidenhead disappear. Presto. Now you see it . . . now you don't. The Pill made chastity disappear, too.

Pandora's box opened and unleashed a curiosity and appetite that wanted to devour as many adventures as it could. To counter it, I got serial boyfriends and used them as chastity belts. They kept me monogamous, sublimating my sex drive in my work. And each ill-fitting relationship ended with a heartbreak that, like this last one, would outlast the love, reconstituting all my inhibitions with a romantic renewal every few lonely, hungry, horny springs.

The image I presented in public was modest—the marrying kind without a kind to marry. Seeming libidinous could ruin my image, I felt. As a late-night comedy girl du jour in the early eighties, I played political wives from Jackie to Rosalynn to Nancy. Sexlessness was a key to those characters.

My grandfatherly gynecologist of many years rushes into the room, "Good to see you," and my maudlin reveries peter out.

I'm very comforted to see him, until he prepares to introduce gadgetry that's glacial in size, sharpness, and temperature into me, and I recall the limits of our relationship.

"Ow?" I remind him of my preference for smaller intrusions.

He withdraws, pats my thigh, gets a friendly, plastic virgin-size speculum. I feel like a plastic virgin, starting all over again, scared to death of everything. Ouch. He's in.

"So, it's been awhile," he says.

Amazing—he can tell just by looking. I guess he knows me down there better than anybody, better than I know myself.

"Are there cobwebs?" I ask.

"I mean, since you've been in the office for a checkup," he says.

Oh. I focus on the clouds painted across the sky-blue ceiling to distract myself.

"So, you've been inactive."

"Celibate two years," I tell the bald head between my knees. "Not because I'm saving myself for marriage. Not because I'm spiritual. Not because I couldn't have sex if I wanted it . . ."

"Uh-huh," he says.

"I'll just never again be intimate. There's no such thing as safe sex. It's nothing but dangerous if you have a heart attached to your vagina."

He withdraws, washes up.

"I never want to love, leave, or get left again," I say. "It's all too painful."

"Well, it's in working order, so"—he squeezes my arm for emphasis—"use it or lose it."

"Use it. To what end?"

"You don't need to get married. Don't look for everything in one package. Have one for talk, one for fun, one for sex. And, until you find them, use this."

He scrawls a note on a prescription slip for a dildo. He's written down the type, the material, and an aspirational size that scares the hell out of me. The horror of looking lusty at a pharmacy overtakes me.

But he writes down the address of the new Hustler store on

the Sunset Strip. Whenever I thought of the Strip, I'd salivate for a roast chicken— a Pavlovian response to my old neighborhood haunt, Greenblatt's. I'd spent many a Saturday night lined up with all the other lonely single women at the deli counter, looking for a fix. Like them, I'd learned to sublimate my rampant sensuality with Greenblatt's hot birds right off the spit.

I'd rush home to raise the entire carcass to my mouth, hot and moist, tearing its succulent skin apart, my gnashing teeth biting, my lips licking, sucking at its humanlike juices. I loved swallowing its surrendering flesh, then biting the bones, crunching and cracking, and slurping out their marrow into my bottomless starvation. I'd make a mess, often eating on the floor in front of the TV in a way I would never be caught dead eating with others. A public outing at the Hustler store might be far worse.

"Are you kidding? What if somebody sees me?"

But with a "Thirty Kegels a day keeps the aging away," he's on to the next pelvis, busy as a bee pollinating all his flowers with suggestions like this.

I look at the paper. I wonder if this is covered by my medical plan. I wonder if he gets kickbacks. Maybe he's joking. I shove it into the debris at the bottom of my purse, but he's got me thinking. Because deep inside this silly little mind, I want to believe that by some fluke I might be able to make love and have love again, that the game ain't over yet. I'm only in the adolescence of old age, after all.

So one day, when I don't feel like eating or reading or crying or socializing but am ready for a slightly braver life, I make my pilgrimage to the Hustler store at the crack of opening. Its official opening isn't until tonight. I figure who would see me there? Who in their right mind that I know would go to a place like that at 9:00 a.m., even for medical reasons? Sure, I'm scared, but it's time to take out insurance on the possibility of future pleasure. Buying a dildo will be a life-affirming act of faith. Kind of like offering a teething ring to get a baby's mouth ready for meat. I park a block away. I'm wearing a trench coat. I put the collar up. I slip on some shades. I walk in the welcoming front door under the fancy marquee, where they're still sanding the floors at the entrance. I stop in my tracks and crumple up the prescription slip in my clammy fist.

This is no apothecary. Nor is this a smarmy sleaze shop for dirty old men. This is a modern, mainstream mall of amazements—an amusement arcade—a shrine to wildness with walls of erotica two stories high. There are novelty items: edible panties, pornographic greeting cards, pacifiers with penises, pencils with breasts for erasers, pickle-shaped peckers, and penile water pistols with balls for triggers. But they've also got serious stuff for any kink you can think of—masks, clamps, pulleys . . . funnels? Any offbeat fantasy, any peccadillo you thought was all yours, baby, they've got an entire wing for it—Bed, Bondage, and Beyond.

This Fellini-esque fairground would be completely shocking if it didn't compel my anthropological curiosity: what do you do with that, where, and to whom? But I have a mission to fulfill. I ask a woman hanging a light where the "massagers" might be. She smirks and points to an entire department of dicks. Every color of the rainbow, any size or sound or substance you can imagine, is on aggressive display. Each brags on its box—some vibrate, some rotate, some migrate, some can be run by remote. Some even come with instructions in Braille. There's the Regular Joe, and there's a kosher cock with descriptions in Hebrew. All friendly members stand at erect attention, promising zipless, fleshless fooling around with no downside. A freckle-faced girl unpacking merchandise asks, like sweetness itself, "Can I help you?"

"Just looking," I say. No crime in looking. I'm getting engrossed, and a bit titillated, too, but more lights are going on in here and they're wheeling equipment up behind me, so I settle on a basic skin-simulating brown model that looks user-friendly. You can even warm it in the microwave, *ON LOW*, it warns. It lives in a nice long box. Its name is Tyrone. I pay, get it brown-bagged, collect myself, and turn around into a blinding bank of spotlights.

"We're rolling," someone says.

It's *Entertainment Tonight* and Larry Flynt is being interviewed in his wheelchair four feet in front of me. That's me in the background sneaking out of range as fast as I can casually run. I'm also seen bolting out the door in the B-roll of the episode—shown at seven, CBS prime time the next night—clutching an oblong bag. In the trench coat and the sunglasses, I could hardly recognize myself, and I didn't think anyone else could, either. And besides, what would a nice Jewish girl like me be doing in a place like that?

At home, things are looking up. Now that I no longer need sanitary pads or other period paraphernalia, there's so much more space under the sink. I make a nice home for my toy boy. Tyrone comes with lubricant, a cleaner, and recommendations for his maintenance. This is the beginning of a beautiful friendship. Maybe I'll get him a brother.

So, it's Thanksgiving week—me and Tyrone are lying around thinking up stuffing recipes—and a friend leaves a message on my answering machine: I am featured in the centerfold of *Star* magazine. Currently voicing a mother and her mother on the hit cartoon *Rugrats*, without any recent personal appearances as myself, I wonder what the hell. I incognito myself over to the supermarket with eggs as an excuse and sidle up to the ten-items-or-less line. I purchase my very first issue of *Star* and rush to my car, poring through to find myself opposite a radiant Carol Burnett, who is on the "Best Dressed" page wearing Chanel at some charity event. And across the fold, on the "Worst Dressed" side, is me in my trench coat and sunglasses, identified at the grand opening of the Hustler store.

I figure few I know will see this. Nobody I know subscribes to *Star*. But it's the holidays, you see, and everyone I've ever known, stuck in long lines at supermarkets, takes advantage of the opportunity to browse the tabloids. Aunts, cousins, producer friends, apparently all shameless closet readers, mail me clippings with congratulations, easing my horror with their nonchalance. Some schmuck even mails it to my mother, who, fortunately, does not even know what the Hustler store is.

"A very nice picture of you," she says, "but what's with the trench coat and dark glasses?"

My manager assures me, "Any press is good press."

My fantasy of preserving an upstanding image until married combusts. I am no longer an ingenue. But what the hell am I now, and how the hell, at this stage and age, have I ended up so alone, holed up with someone like Tyrone?

THE PRICE OF POPULAR

In grammar school, I sat alone at lunch. At auditorium assemblies, I was always stuck at the end of the row, never near the middle where the popular girls sat.

Nobody in my neighborhood liked me much. I was a little nervous. I was a little Jewish. I was a little gifted. I was a little sickly. I was mostly chosen last for teams. I talked too fast, felt sad inside, and tried to hide it. I tried to act like other people looked like they felt.

In junior high, I joined chorus and got good at harmonizing. Other kids looked at me interestedly. Maybe they didn't really like me more. Maybe they just needed to get their alto note from me. I still sat alone at lunch near where the trays and trash were thrown. I sang a solo line in the Thanksgiving performance for the entire school in the big auditorium.

"Very good singing!" said Miss Rudnick. I was happy for weeks.

Seventh-grade Valentine's Day, a folded-up piece of paper was sticking out of my locker vent with a red heart crayoned onto it. When I got valentines, my name was always spelled incorrectly, so I braced myself. I unfolded it to find a note written in good penmanship with my name spelled correctly. It told me I was pretty and had a good voice, and it liked my hair. It told me its author was someone I didn't know but who liked me and would write again soon. It was signed, *from Your Secret Admirer.*

My scalp and the hairs on my arms prickled, and I looked around to see if anyone was watching, but people were rushing by to class. Maybe this wasn't a joke. Maybe somebody liked me. I felt different now, in a good way. I felt less alone walking down the hall. My back felt cozy, like when my grandmother would hold me in her lap against her big chest. I stood outside history class, ignoring the bell, reading the note again.

In history I felt self-conscious. *Is he here?* I wondered. I peeked around, but no one looked at me. *If he is here, he is a very good pretender,* I thought. In chorus singing "I Feel Pretty" from *West Side Story,* I noticed I did have a nice voice and I did feel pretty, and I wondered if he heard me or saw me, so I looked around, but nobody was looking at me. All were busy reading their rhythms. I sang the harmony prouder and louder, and Miss Rudnick smiled at me more, and I felt happier.

That night I lay awake wondering, *Who can it be? Is he on Student Council? In 11:00 a.m. study hall? Will he be my first boyfriend? Will we hold hands in the halls like the popular kids?* But the next day, there was no note, and none the day after that, either. I had an ache in my stomach. *Maybe he doesn't like me anymore,* I thought, *or maybe I did something wrong. Maybe he saw the gigantic pimple reddening my whole chin.* But two days later, there was another note sticking out, with a picture of a yellow sun crayoned on it. Happiness fluttered in my stomach.

The note said he had been out for two days with a cold but that thinking of me had made him happy. It was again signed, *from Your Secret Admirer.* I tried to remember who was absent from which classes but couldn't think of a boy I might like who might like me who'd been out. I held the note open as I walked to class, feeling more confident than ever before. I really wanted someone else to see, someone to know. My cheeks grew hot from possible eyes.

I read the note over and over in class, wondering if my secret admirer and I would someday grow up and get married, and the girl next to me noticed and after class asked me what the note was. I took a chance and showed her. She got all excited, took it, and showed her girlfriend, who asked bluntly who it was from.

"I don't know," I said, enjoying her interest.

They told two other kids, and all looked at me more often.

Next day, no note, and not for two more days. The girls were losing interest. I began feeling unconfident again. But on a Friday, a note with a picture of an apple appeared, folded in my locker vent. As I read, others joined me and were looking over my shoulder, and I let them. *Popularity is more important than privacy,* I thought. In the new note he told me he liked me, and he liked apples second best.

The girls and now one boy exclaimed:

"I wonder who it is?"

"We have to find out!"

"Somebody who likes apples, hmm . . . "

It is a puzzle, I thought, *and I am the mystery girl at the center, and I like this immensely.*

Now I had three girls for company at my lunch table near the tray stacks and trash, and we watched each lunch tray go by to see who maybe had an apple. Suspense was heavy among us. Almost everybody took an apple back to class that day, and we guessed, "Maybe him? Maybe him?" We laughed and laughed together. I had never laughed much with others, since my father said I had a stupid-sounding hyena laugh, but now my hyena laugh made them all laugh harder, like maybe they liked me.

My Secret Admirer left another folded-up note with a tree on it. He told me he would leave me a hint at the oak tree I passed on my way home from school. I was thrilled that a lot of girls and boys would walk me to the tree to see. We ran up to the oak tree to see a newly carved musical note with my initials in it.

"He must be in music class or chorus!"

"Maybe it's Mr. Arpaia, the music teacher!" screeched one girl, and we laughed and laughed together. If it was, you'd never know it. Mr. Arpaia only admired the boys.

On Monday, my Secret Admirer left a note that on Friday he would walk by my lunch table at 12:50 p.m. and smile, then bite his apple. If I liked him, I should smile back. I felt thrilled. I felt scared.

On that important day, several girls and guys sat at nearby tables to watch me watching the trays.

At 12:49 on the cafeteria clock, I felt like I might throw up; my jaw ached from clenching my molars. A hush fell over the entire lunchroom, not just the tables near me. The bell rang, and a bunch of students brought trays toward the trash area; several had apples. This felt like watching a quiz show, waiting for the answer to be revealed. Tension was high as two apple boys approached, dumped their trash, and kept their apples for later. Then a tall black-haired boy in a band sweater rose from a remote table behind us with an apple on his tray and circled around. *No, not him,* I thought. Albert Altschuler played the tuba and triangle in the marching band and school orchestra, and his playing was excellent. But he was not popular, and I knew I might not be popular anymore if I liked him and said I liked him. Albert cleared and put his tray away, then turned back, looking directly toward me. I saw nervousness in his eyes as he took a big bite of the apple.

I was aware that pandemonium had broken out in the cafeteria, and the girls looked at me and screamed, and I smelled spaghetti sauce on my plate, which was good a minute ago and now smelled like garbage. I heard myself screaming, too, as I saw Albert's neck pulling inside his band sweater shoulders like a turtle as he fast-walked out. I felt I might explode as people yelled and poked at me.

"It's Albert Altschuler!"

"He's a junior who stayed back!"

"Albert is your Secret Admirer!"

"Albert wants you as a girlfriend!"

"Do you like him?! Do you like him?!"

I couldn't feel. I couldn't tell if I would like him. Maybe if no one was watching me, I would be happy he liked me and would even maybe like him back.

I couldn't feel anything at all, except at that moment I knew how it felt to be popular.

And I knew how it felt to be cruel.

GRAY AREAS

As a kid it was hard for me to tell the difference between appropriate and inappropriate, between funny and warped, as black comedy was my family's antidote to despair. They were an easy crowd—with a few pratfalls and funny noises, I could move my elders from festering depressed in their Jewish horrors to giggles of hysteria.

My father thrived on pranks, adding slapstick into every interaction he could. Ridiculing my mother, belittling my sister, making gibes and jokes at my expense—this was hilarious for him, and for his father and father-in-law. It was not so funny for the females, whose smiles were more like winces.

"Get a load of them," Dad would chortle. "They got no sense of humor!"

When my sister and I were little, my dad bought a small prefab house, near the very first amusement park in the US. Savin Rock had an enormous roller coaster, on which people had actually been killed, and scary clowns selling strange foods that stained your face and stuck to your shoes. It had arcades, shooting galleries, stock car races, and lowlifes hosting floating crap games. Dad loved to take us there to show us off to his bookie, who ran a ball toss booth on the side. We'd clamor for rides on the merry-go-round's life-size horses, tugging at Dad's sleeves for dimes.

"C'mon, what's the point of ponies if I can't bet on 'em to win place or show?" he'd grouse. And when we sometimes did take a spin, he'd cheat by lifting us off the horses to grab the brass rings and win prizes. Finally, he got caught, and we were banished from the amusement park until the owner died and Dad reclaimed it.

My mother's tastes in entertainment were far more sophisticated. She'd fill the house with music from classical radio stations and opera and musical theater albums, singing and dancing along to Al Jolson and Jimmy Durante tunes to crack up my father and my little sister, Norma.

I remember one winter night—when Norma was four and I was eight—we were famished waiting for Daddy to sit down to supper. He was busy watching football and on the phone, betting a buck a point with his bookie. After nagging for an hour, Mom resorted to extreme measures. She stripped off her clothes and stood in front of the TV screen naked, trilling Gilbert and Sullivan to drown out the sports scores.

> *"I am a maiden, cold and stately,*
> *Heartless I, with a face divine.*
> *What do I want with a heart, innately?*
> *Ev'ry heart I meet is mine,*
> *Ev'ry heart I meet is mine, is mine!"*

Her nude parts bounced around, shimmying in front of my father's face.

Norma and I were horrified. "Mommy, put your clothes on and please *stop singing!*"

My father let her go on for a minute. I could see a gleam brewing in his eyes, feel the roil building in his belly.

"Yeah, hang on a second, Marty," he said into the phone. Then he threw down the receiver, grabbed Mom, and, chortling like a loon as she screamed, shoved her out the front door into the winter cold. He locked it and told us to go eat.

She started ringing the doorbell, tapping at the windows, yelling, then pleading. My sister and I were hysterical—crying, frightened, peeking through the curtains at her.

"Daddy, let her in!" we screamed.

"Don't look at her—let's just go eat, pretend she's not there," he giggled.

"That's not funny!" we shrieked. It was cold out. She might die. Worse yet, the neighbors might see her. The tapping stopped.

"Mommy froze," wept Norma.

"Daddy, let her *in*!" I yelled.

"What, you're on her side now? I pay for the food around here. Shut up and eat."

I felt like we were naked in the cold, too. If I couldn't rescue my mother, how could she ever rescue us back? He followed us into the kitchen and eyeballed us as we tried to stomach all this, then took his food back to the game. We were prisoners of an awful war. I force-fed my food into my mouth, chomped, gagged, couldn't swallow, felt like I'd throw up. Norma felt sick, too. Pretending I had to pee, I spat it all out in the toilet, then peered out the side window. Mom was shivering in the DeSoto with a blanket. As soon as he was on the phone again, I let her in the back door, shaking as much as she was.

"Are you okay, Mommy?" asked Norma.

Mom was white, the dots in the middle of her breasts sticking out red, her possum bristling black hairs down there. I couldn't look. I could feel the helplessness in her, terror in my sister, and rage in me. But she laughed, tough, like it was all a big joke, defiant so we wouldn't be scared. We tried to laugh, too—figured as long as we could laugh, life was okay.

Our home was an "abusement park," where teasing took the place of affection, rough-housing took the place of hugs, pokes replaced pats, and funhouse mirrors distorted our images of ourselves. My sister and I hung onto the wild ride of our parents' marriage wearing clown faces till we could hardly recognize our own.

The summer that Norma was eleven and I was fifteen, on the weekends Daddy would bring his poker buddies—I called them Sleepy, Dopey, Slimy, Fatty, Creepy, Snotty, and Doc—into the yard where she and I sunbathed in our swimsuits many a day trying to tan the backs of our legs. The men would gaze at us like we were part of the landscape, complimenting my father on how well we were shaping up. He'd get out his camera out and coax me to do cheesecake poses.

Norma's dots were just budding; mine were blooming breasts, and my pale possum was sprouting hairs down there. We were beyond self-conscious. We'd roll ourselves up in the beach blanket and hobble away as the men all howled. But that repeating peepshow scenario stayed with me. I got triple vision seeing the men through my own eyes, seeing myself through their eyes, and seeing my father seeing them and me through his eyes. The approval embarrassed me but turned me on, too. Their eye tracks lingered like touches on my flesh, and I was titillated and ashamed.

In high school I learned to Frug and do the Slop with soul from groovy Black boys. Improvising cool moves to Motown without a partner made much more sense to me than being shoved around by klutzy guys in waltzes and Cha-Chas. Shaking it up and making it up felt sexy.

I learned early that I could monopolize men's attention for profit till I was qualified to earn it with brains, talent, and good character. I made my first respectable money go-go dancing at local clubs and mixers. If I hadn't had that currency early on, my feeling of imprisonment, deprivation, and indignity might have been intolerable. I was brokering my body to fight the suppression of my soul. I got off on having as many men as possible attracted to me. I felt really good and really bad about feeling this good, but I figured I'd postpone thinking deeply about it till I was older and smarter.

As I got starter jobs in comedy sketches, I often found myself the butt and breast of the jokes. Old-time male comics liked to play the victim as some dame strutted her sexy stuff across the stage. That got less funny as brilliant brownette stand-ups like Elayne Boosler capsized the nightly male lineups at the comedy clubs with laughable truths. I developed self-deprecating characters who'd embody the confusions of women and the lewd behaviors of men, as I found the funny for myself in stand-up. It took a while for men to stop being squeamish and to truly laugh at gifted female comics.

Boy, did old-time comic Henny Youngman's "Take my wife, please" bits make my Dad laugh. Henny's jokes were Dad's favorite catchphrases when he wanted to demean my mother. It was quite the kick for Dad when Henny and I appeared together on a live TV show in 1980.

So, as the end credits rolled, I held a mic, thanking him and the live audience for being with us, and chummy Henny put his arm around me. But Henny's hand didn't stop at my back. No, no. Its fingers crawled onward, landing on the side of my left breast, two inches past my underarm but a world away from proper—and he knew it.

Uninvited tickles in erogenous areas have never touched my funny bone, but his hand had a weird sense of humor, with his insolent fingers lingering on me, pinned under my arm, wiggling like worms, and a lot of the live audience saw. In a split second my primitive impulses got negated by others. I wanted to pull away, but we were going out live unedited. I wanted to call him out but had no witty rejoinder in mind. I wanted to slap him, but he was old and might croak. I slammed my upper arm down to halt further invasion, holding the mic, doing my spiel, trying to hold it together, spasming.

I covered until the cameras panned away, then spun to glare at him. He held my gaze, and centuries of male entitlement and female indignation duked it out between us. Then he broke, winked, and stepped away into his entourage as I fumed.

Mom told me that when Daddy heard about and replayed the struggle over and over again on his video recorder, he just howled at what a slimy old letch Henny was, copping a cheap feel off his daughter.

■

In my forties, I thought I'd finally scrubbed clear my murkiest gray areas in therapy, ironed out the kinks, separated my lights from my darks, tweezed apart cultural norms from biological instincts. Some of my survival behaviors morphed from shameful to understandable and forgivable. I affirmed that my unpaternal father prioritizing gambling and his cronies' jollies over the security of his girls was narcissistic and perverted. Still, gray areas continued to fog my thinking.

I recall emceeing What a Pair, an annual fundraiser starring glamorous female singing duos and their great bodies that benefited breast cancer research. I remember all us girls accepting a swag bag with pink Playboy Bunny slippers that night from Hugh Hefner, a big benefactor. He owed breasts big-time, had made his fortune on them. In our push-up bras and tight gowns, we were the perps and producers of the event, with a wink—the willing subjects of ogling for a good cause, and we felt just fine about selling ourselves out for the culturally enlivening evening.

■

In 2017 in the very same week that waves of Weinstein accusations were flooding the news, I attended a charity gala to raise money for homeless single mothers. Ed Asner, who I knew from shared play readings and social events, was being honored. I hugged and congratulated him for a recent TV turn as a letch, and for earning the Helping Hands Humanitarian Award that evening. And as we posed for press photos, he rested one of his helping hands on my behind.

Certainly, amid recently exposed affronts, this was minor, more in the familial realm of Al Franken's playful pats and pinches than any Cosby crimes. But my head spun with questions. Was this flirting, flattering, was Ed challenging the newly forming status quo? Had I provoked him by gushing about his triumphs while wearing a too-tight dress? Perhaps he thought his age and venerability and my admiration gave him get-out-of-jail-free latitude. I wondered if he did this with all the women who posed with him that night, but watching closely, I saw no glimmers on faces indicating that other asses had gotten grabbed. Maybe we'd all gotten too good over the decades at camouflaging, at smiling during shock, and it needed to get flushed out of the brush so we could all finally see it.

That same evening as modestly dressed actor Marion Ross was onstage at the mic praising Ed's many achievements in the arts, his heroic stand for justice, he limped up slowly on his now constantly used cane and stood, first flush behind her, then right up against her. He buried his face intimately in her hair. She rushed through her words, tossed him his award, and fled the stage. And then he spoke soberly about the organization's support of homeless single mothers, and his support for getting women out of poverty. Four hundred baffled attendees applauded Ed Asner's philanthropy, hoping he'd throw in a cogent statement about flirting at this new bleeding edge of #MeToo. But he left the stage and left us all in the dark.

■

Strolling on a beach at the edge of the Adriatic in Italy one Sunday afternoon, I was thrilled to see toy buckets and shovels and pebbles taking precedence over cell phones for the little bathers. Watchful parents and I nodded to each other, sharing the international feeling of gratitude at children's play. A little girl, maybe two and a half years old, wearing a clearly beloved tutu over her bathing suit, was making a mud pie near my feet. She met my eyes shyly. I beamed, pointing to her pink tulle.

"What a pretty skirt you have!" I said in English.

With confident cool, she gave me a flirtatious little flounce of her skirt, waggled her little hips, and splashed away. This toddler was working major coquette moves.

Was this a socialized or an instinctive behavior? Pondering what the hell might be on Italian TV and who the local role models might be, I looked to her matronly mother, who was sitting on a blanket in her church finest, golden crucifix on her chest. We'd both raised our eyebrows in amazement. I queried telepathically, "Where did she get that?"

Her mother gazed at her daughter, who, after tagging a little boy, was running away squealing in a frenzy of femininity. Mamma shrugged her shoulders and eyebrows at me, as if to say, "I have no idea."

And yet we did.

Together we gazed at this little girl, wondering how she'd navigate the gray areas.

THE CROSSROADS

I spritzed with the Sears glass cleaner. I scrubbed with the Sears-labeled cloth. The scum on the glass shelf atop the rack of girls' separates reshaped itself like an ornery amoeba.

It rolled, surrendered its edge a smidge, but would not let go—just like my dream of acting stuck to my every single waking thought, and my dreams at night, too. I slid the preteen torso mannequin, its budding breasts tamed inside a plaid Sears junior girls one-piece, over the snotty gook to hide it.

Every worker in this shiny, empty new store was trying to look as busy bee as me to justify their pointless positions. And this aspiring actress, pretending to be a scrubber/salesgirl in the juniors department for the summer, was getting a sore throat from the smell of starch and ammonia-laced solvent. And a headache from the plaid polyester separates. Or a cough. Or maybe tuberculosis. After four days on the job, I was already rehearsing how I'd convince the stuffy store manager I needed a sick day. I could moan and rasp my voice on cue. I could cry. I counted down the seconds to my half-hour lunch break, then excused myself to my coworker, who was killing time straightening small, medium, and large tags until her break.

There had been seventy applicants for eight entry-level summer sales jobs at this shiny new Sears, which had just opened at the intersection of sleepy Bull Hill Lane and the bustling Boston Post Road. Since the Armstrong Rubber Company had closed down, taking with it many small soda fountains and luncheonettes that serviced it, there hadn't been a new business with new jobs in the area for years. This modern new Sears and its automotive department was the town trophy. The prize. They hosted a tour of it the first week it was open. People took pictures.

"You're lucky to get the damned job—plus benefits! It's a great company," said my father. "And you're sixteen, kiddo. Time to get serious, work for a living like the rest of us."

Sentenced. To life at work. To a prison of monotony eight hours a day. After my thrilling experience playing a small singing role in Yale's undergraduate Drama Club production of *The Threepenny Opera*, this felt like cruel punishment. I had beat out a bunch of other townies—no women undergraduates were enrolled at Yale—and got the coveted turn acting with terrific male actors. I had gotten big laughs and mentions in the reviews. I got taken to the Yale prom by one of the stars. To me, this proved I had a future in theater. To my father, this was like a high school hobby that I should get over. He, who had never kept a job with anyone in his whole life, preferring to have his own business failures selling aluminum siding and home improvements on the phone from home. It would have been a big home improvement if my father had gone to a real job.

I strolled backstage past workers shaking lint out of crisp new clothes—they were restocking, replacing the many swimsuits and short sets sold over the Memorial Day weekend. After a week working here, I could get a 20 percent discount on a polka dot bathing suit with a skirt Mom had pointed out. Whoopee.

I just made it to the ladies' locker room, where I relaxed in the too-disinfected stall and sucked on a paper cut I'd gotten thumbing through the new Sears catalogue. What else was there to do to get through the four hours looming ahead, which were certain to be as horribly boring and uneventful as the three hours behind? I found a dime in my pocket. My mother always told me to carry dimes to make emergency calls and to wear good underpants. I was wearing new Sears underpants, with good elastic and no stains and no cotton, and I had a dime, too. I figured I'd use it to call her from the Sears warehouse to kill a few more of my remaining minutes, spring her slightly from her own job trap at Pitney Bowes Postage Meters a few miles down the road.

Her hello was evasive; the phone line seemed to vibrate with her nerves. Ho boy. Another fight with my father?

"Well, no," she said. "We got a call last night from the director of the play at Yale."

"What? He called?" A shock ran through my ribs. *Threepenny Opera* had been a big hit, and my virgin prostitute turn in the production got me noticed for a funny little walk and voice I made up to sing Kurt Weill's lush score.

"Your father and I discussed it and decided you should stay at Sears for the summer, until you go off to college in September."

"What? Wait! Discussed what? Decided?"

"Oh," she tossed off, "the New London Opera Company is renting the production from Yale to put on at their theater for three weekends in July, Fridays, Saturdays, Sundays."

"Yeah? Yeah?"

"And they asked permission for you to come to New London and reprise your role."

I could hardly squeak, "Really?"

"But Daddy says you'll lose the Sears job if you take three

Fridays off. And he's probably right."

My stomach had a shooting pain.

"So I said, 'At least she'd make a little money from doing the show, and they'll give her room and board,' and he said, 'She needs to work a hell of a lot longer than that to get money for college,' and I said—"

"Ma!" I screeched as the passing manager gave me the hairy eyeball.

"Look, I know you want to be an actress, I wanted to be a singer—but we can't have everything we want just because we want it, y'know."

I was not convinced this was so. She had been brainwashed by my father, like the guy in *The Manchurian Candidate* movie.

"I've got to go back to work. We'll talk when you pick me up."

I'd bought my father's big-finned old DeSoto from him with the money I saved from being a go-go girl at mixers and Bar Mitzvahs plus babysitting. I felt pretty powerful in that car, dragging with the Yalies on the turnpike, proud that I'd bought it with my own earnings. Dad's deal was I had to pick my mother up after work to save him the trouble. Sometimes I wanted to just run off with her, take Route 1 and follow it as far as it would go forever, past Florida and Cuba, away from my father, and take my sister, too.

Unwrapping my pasty salami-on-white in the locker room, burping a Sprite I got from the machine, eating too fast out of frustration, I could feel my intestines twisting. I was at a major crossroads—my destiny, unmapped and unknown, versus my Dad's plan, known, dreaded, and a dead-end.

I drifted in my mind back to being little, when he was my hero, my deity. I'd clamber into his lap on his throne, and he'd let me light his cigarette. He'd stick a Camel in his mouth, steady my grip on the lighter, support my thumb on the rough-hewn little wheel, and help me spin it till it sparked, till a pretty blue flame erupted. I'd raise it to the tip of his cigarette, and the end would light up orange in response, and smoke would come up. How I loved setting my daddy on fire, then lying against his chest as he made smoke rings in the air. I'd be awed by their ghostlike floating in suggestive circles, delighted at how they'd disappear into thin air, just like soap bubbles he waved from a wand into the sky that hovered twinkling above my head. I could make things disappear with one finger and felt very powerful back then.

Now sixteen, I wished I could make him disappear. Post-puberty, pre-college, pre-everything except gigantic wishes to get out of our house and town, I was stuck dependent on him for a few more years until I graduated college. And as long as I was there, he expected respect—even fake respect. He wanted me to salute and say "yessir" like a soldier. In his mind, I was a puny nobody in his platoon who should obey orders to pull my weight to earn my room and board. Dad demanded to be loved and kissed on the cheek each night at bedtime. My sister always did, but she still loved him like I had at her size. Faking affection like my mother did made me feel sick and confused. I wanted them to love each other. I wanted to love them. I wanted so much more than my folks had ever chosen for themselves. I felt that if I lived like them, I would die.

I trudged back to the juniors department and tagged out my coworker for her break. I started clock-watching, then minute-hand-watching, then watching the little red lines on the clockface get swept in shadow. One hundred minutes to my next break. Dust the cash register, ninety-nine now. Greet a customer, ninety-eight. I might not make it. I might go mad first.

As I rang up pastel waist-high underpants like mine for a mother and her daughters and made teensy talk about where they were in school and what colors they liked, as if I cared—boy was I good at acting—my brain was whirling around this new possibility, this potential date with destiny, with a professional opera company! Mom sneaking me to a few singing lessons was paying off.

At breakfast my father hadn't even mentioned the director. Now I was really, really mad. He'd say I had no right to be mad, but I was—oh, I was. Wasn't it my right to know I had a job offer—an acting job offer? This was my real feeling, not a pretend feeling like he preferred. Wasn't it my right to be *furious*? My enormous feelings would be welcome in the theater, but not at home. I did not want to pretend I wasn't upset, like so many other times when I made like everything was okay, lumping my throat, burning my stomach. I wanted a life in the theater, where my enormous feelings would be welcome, as they were not welcome at home.

I stumbled through the day, my head aching, my throat getting more sore, coughing in front of my coworker a lot for emphasis, for an alibi. I got my purse, clocked out, picked up my mother at work. She knew from my face and my three-Kleenex crying not to say one word all the way home. I marched up the stairs of our front stoop ahead of her, approaching the guillotine with courage and dignity. I threw open the aluminum screen door. My sister could always tell by my face if she should make herself scarce and headed to our room to hide. Usually I'd try to charm and distract and mollify him with funny faces and schtick. If we could make him laugh, sometimes we got out of jail free. But my sense of humor was unavailable.

"I'm going," I said, facing down his ferocity, which was seething at me like a cartoon bull from his BarcaLounger throne. "I know this is what I'm supposed to do in my life, not work at Sears."

He scoffed, stomped, spewed, snorted about the money, the fruitlessness of an acting job that would lead nowhere, nowhere at all.

"Hey," he said, "you don't know anything. If you quit Sears, they'll never hire you back next summer or the summer after! You'll be out of a job. And you owe me, kid, for your room and board all these years."

"Hal . . . ," whined my mother

"You stay out of it." He wagged a finger at her, then turned back to me. "How are you gonna take care of me when I get old if you can't take care of yourself? You think I'm gonna support this acting craziness? Who the hell do you think you are, Shirley Temple?"

My mother cowered on the couch. The night before, we had cozied, bonding in her bed, watching *Gaslight*, a movie about a man who lies and tries to drive a woman crazy. My father always made my mother believe she couldn't do anything right, that she was weak, dumb, and helpless without him. She never disagreed. She'd even let him take my dog away, my beloved puppy I bought at the pound when I was eight that he said she'd been nuts to let me have in the first place. I was told that my dog had nipped and scratched a neighbor's kid in play and that the neighbors had called the warden. Dad said he'd rescued my dog from the dog catcher in the nick of time and driven it to live on a friend's farm many miles away, where it would run around free and happy. At the time, I'd screamed, so great was my heartbreak.

"It's just a dog, kiddo. What the hell's wrong with you? How come you didn't cry this much when Grandpa died? He loved you!" he said.

I didn't love Grandpa. He used to grab the middle of my face, put his thumb between his fingers, and say: "I got your no-ose!" like I was too dumb to see the thumbnail sticking out from between his nicotine-stained fingers. He stunk of old-man smell, and my mother told me she didn't like him, either, because he was mean to my sweet Grandma Molly, poking her, calling her fat, until she died young to get out of it. I remember I loved the feeling of Grandma and her hugs the short time I knew her, and my dog licked and kissed and played and made us laugh, and I loved him ferociously. I was mixed up about Mom. I mostly felt sorry for her. Was that love?

I consoled myself thinking that my puppy would have lots of animal playmates on the farm, but nobody could love him as deeply as I did. But watching *Gaslight* with my mother, it hit me: We didn't know anybody who knew anybody with a farm—my father had no friends. There weren't any farms near us, and my father would never have wasted gas and time driving anywhere to take my dog anyplace. My father had gaslighted me, and my mother confirmed it that night. My dog had been taken back to the warden and probably died in the pound, just because he'd played too puppy-hard one day.

My father was betraying me again now. He wanted to break my spirit, like trainers did in all those horse books I read. I always identified with the wild horse, rearing up, whinnying. My mother was broken in but good. I would not be.

"Dad," I said, summoning my ambition, my wishes, my belief, my defiant nostrils flaring like the Black Stallion's, stomping at the ground. "I'm going!"

First, he puffed up big, then hissed like a balloon losing air. He stared at me full face, assessing my guts, my gumption. My mother was telling him to calm down.

"You stay out of this—I pay your rent, too," he sneered at her, then he sneered back at me and threw up his hands.

"What the hell. Go! But when this cockamamie career doesn't work out, don't come cryin' to me."

I trembled. Then I packed. I called in sick to Sears. I'd call in to quit once I figured stuff out. My mother drove me to the railway station in my DeSoto the next morning and bought me a ticket. This would be the first time I'd ever stayed overnight away from home and her. I'd spend three four-day weekends at Mitchell College's dorms, and I was nervous. But then I noticed she was crying, and my pang of sympathy was bigger than my fear. I'd be brave for my mother. I wondered if she would miss me, if she'd be jealous. I told her I wanted her to run away from home with me that very minute.

"Why don't you divorce him, Mom?" I pleaded. "He's so mean to you, to all of us."

"I know. I've thought about it," she said. "But I can't. Not yet. Your sister's too young, and I don't have enough money from my job—he keeps all our money in his bank account."

She was stuck in the bad luck that was my father's life: his ill health, his temper, his gambling habit, his miserly ways. I was surprised and relieved she was thinking about it, planning it. I hoped she would escape as soon as she could and take my sister with her. I hoped I'd have a good home and a good heart for them to come to. She squeezed my hand as we parted at the ticket window and said, "You go. Good luck."

And she turned away. She didn't look back.

As I boarded the train, I loved her more, for letting me go this way, than I ever had before. I feared for my sister without me there to draw fire from his rages. I felt scared, selfish, brave, angry, and proud—all at the same time.

Watching out the train window, clackety clacking past the backsides of stores and people's yards, I said good-bye to Sears, my hometown, and my father, sad for my mother and sister. Then I thought of the new work to come.

And I couldn't look back.

AN EARNEST PURSUIT

It was a secret between me and me that I kept for years before I even knew what it was or the words for it.

I was addicted to masturbation before I knew about sex, before I even got my first period. I was amazing at it. I didn't know what it meant or the possible repercussions. I thought I might pay a price. I thought I'd probably be punished if they found out. But I needed to escape, and it made me feel good inside. It made me feel good, even though I felt my feeling so good would prove to be very bad. I awaited my fate. I was thrilled that I could give myself such secret pleasure, put myself under such a magical spell.

One day in eighth grade, our health teacher told us girls the technical truth about babies' origins. She had diagrams and drawings and an Invisible Woman with plastic removeable organs. She also had a picture of a penis. I had seen my father's little one in the shower. This one in the science picture was bigger and sticking out. Our teacher showed us illustrations of how the bottom parts of a man matched up like a jigsaw puzzle piece with a woman's underside in intercourse. This arrangement was to be avoided until we were married.

No problem, I thought to myself, queasy. Everything about it looked like it would hurt and lead to worse pain, like the big fat swelling up, then the shoving-hard-screaming-bloody-murder part when a baby was coming out.

I recalled what my poor mother had told me: "Babies come from a husband kissing a wife's belly button." I figured no one had ever taken the time to show her the Invisible Woman's vagina and the Invisible Man's penis. However, back then I was not about to correct her misunderstanding. She was too fragile.

I never made any connection between my paroxysms of pleasure and the roughhousing brats yelling in the halls, yanking our hair. Horses were my turn-ons, especially with topless, saddle-free Indians on them, pumping their pelvises, whooping their war cries. It could make a girl feel good just watching them gallop and rear up and buck. I couldn't wait to get a real horse between my legs. But the first time I sat on one, it was not a comfortable fit, not at all pleasurable as I had imagined. I was stunned, bewildered that what looked like it felt so good to one area—my eyes—was so painful to another, my pleasure place. It was like when I sipped my mother's best-smelling perfume, with a side of delicious-looking chewy red cork Chinese checkers, and had to get my stomach pumped. My senses could deceive me. I would have to be more careful.

Male approval felt essential for my survival in those days. But Dad's dictatorial demands for obedience and my provincial town's emphasis on conformity ignited in me a hunger for independence. I craved freedom from adults' rules and equality with boys long before feminists bared their breasts at protests.

As I matured and menstruated, the tides made a mystical turn. I began to understand boys' appeal. Till then, even the germy spit sharing of kissing in cars after school made me nauseous. Now, the dilemma of being a good girl versus being bold and free, like boys, was tormenting me. What cruel tricks Nature played on girls, inciting urges for abandon that could make us prisoners of out-of-control boys and earn us the condemnation of a puritanical New England society. The scales were tipped against us, and we needed all the wiles and wisdom we could muster to manipulate men and our mothers, to dodge bullets and succeed in the wider world. For me, appearing to be "the marrying kind," wholesome and pure, seemed to be the most advantageous posture. Males were respectful and girls felt unthreatened if I acted oblivious to my sudden physical appeal, suppressing my wanton urge to turn boys on, hiding my secret adventures with Indians that played out under the blanket at night.

While I excelled at being expressive in English studies and Drama Club plays at an early age, I was inhibited in life—sensuous in private, goofy in the social realm. At sixteen, I'd played a prostitute way before I even had breasts. I sang and sashayed and flaunted my scrawny self on stage, then, after the show, I tried to avoid the handsome chemistry professor staying on the same dark dorm hallway.

"Hey there, girl. Saw the show again tonight, and you were even prettier." My body liked his attention, but my mind knew his approval could trick me. My real-life self didn't dress and walk provocatively; it was scared of going all the way into an unknown trap my mind might never escape.

Then, while I was a freshman in college, I learned a new pleasure beyond my imaginings and fears. It came from junior drama major Ernest. With his thick, shiny black hair and eyes that shone from his heart, his pats on my head made me want to pat back. It was the first time I was physically attracted to a really nice man who already had beard ability. We sang opposite each other in the musical version of Oscar Wilde's *The Importance of Being*

Earnest, a show called *Earnest in Love*. We sure were. Playing the leads in the main-stage production of *Romeo and Juliet* conspired to further entrance us. Compelled to move beyond acting and flirting, we were soon embracing behind the scenes.

Princely Ernest, two years older than me, came courting me in classical ways. He'd sweep me away from campus in his cherry-red Alfa Romeo to his little apartment by the sea, where we neglected our homework for intense, sensuous, unconsummated weekends. His approval, his fingers, and, most amazing of all, his tongue, articulate in its speaking of poetry and its shape-shifting dexterity, created more magic carpet rides in my body than I ever dreamed possible. He pleased all my senses, and we went slow enough to enjoy each stop along the way for weeks.

His externally applied caresses put self-inflicted orgasms behind me. With Ernest at the helm, and with the pounding Atlantic erasing my fears, I could relax. I could lose control. I didn't have to play all the parts in my repertory company of private rapture. As layers of role-playing faded away, so did my headaches from concentrating so hard on imaginary horses and Indians kidnapping me and tying me up—so did my hand cramps from self-pleasuring.

Ernest became synonymous with ecstasy. No one had ever felt like he made me feel. I surrendered into my starring role as desired girl, as I orchestrated kissing Ernest to the strains of Tchaikovsky's *Romeo and Juliet* all night long. That music amplified our longing and predicted our ending.

It was the danger that made those spring nights all the more arousing. I knew, lost as I was in his love, that my ambitions to be on Broadway would be endangered if I opened up to the full-throttle manual power of my first man who had hair on his chest and chin. I intuited that my needy heart's attachment could spell doom for me. I had never been caressed and gentled and held since my bosomy, cuddly grandma died, except by Ernest in this very different way.

"But I don't want to go all the way until I get married," I told him one entangled night as we inched closer and closer.

I wasn't sure I meant that entirely. It was a stall technique until I could articulate a more original expression of my reluctance.

"Oh." Chastened, Ernest pulled back. He never brought up that technical last barrier between us, except metaphorically in Shakespearean sonnets. In all honesty, I wasn't quite clear on how integrating Ernest's insistent penis into my body could possibly make things any better than they already were. I was transfixed just petting my first Romeo's beautiful face with its beard capability, feeling smug at my power to create wet spots on his pants.

What sorcery lurked through that hidden door that so many girls my age had already entered, survived, and, since the advent of the Pill, celebrated? It seemed very important to men's bodies, and I so desperately needed Ernest's love that I began to consider marrying him, surrendering my maidenhood, and conceding everything else I ever had in my dreams. I wanted to hoard him, seduce him away from all the other libidinous sirens into captivity in my undulating ship's hold.

Spring of my freshman year, with a three-month separation looming ahead, time felt like it was running out. I was off to be the ingenue in an Equity summer stock musical theater season in the Catskills. He was working crew and playing small roles in a star package touring Massachusetts. Our paths would not cross again until September, and our hearts were anguished in anticipation. It was time to seek women's counsel, as I was never able to do with my repressed mother. I threw myself on the lap of female mercy for the first time.

My dormmates were shocked to learn that, precocious as I seemed, I had never gone all the way, especially with earnest Ernest. Liz, my womanly, wise next-door neighbor, seeking her master's in psychology before I even knew what psychology was, took it upon herself to be my adviser. For a start, she taught me how to use tampons, explaining how roomy it was in there, directing me on insertion from outside my ladies' room stall, like landing a small plane from the tower. The tampon was dry and unfriendly, but after it went in, she was right, I didn't feel it, until I dislodged it by pulling on its string. Amazing. There was room for things up there after all.

Having leaped over that first hurdle, she got me to consider that inside me there was room for both pleasure from penises and my personal sense of power. She urged me into her style of tight capris, fitted jerseys, and kitten heels. But I was a drama major studying the classics and preferred my long skirts as a badge of timeless feminine specialness. I covered myself up in character, as I felt so ordinary and amorphous as myself.

Then Liz began to broach men and lovemaking. And as she had done it every which way with many, she knew lots. I told her how my mother had been skittish about anything to do with intercourse as she had been forced into it rather violently on the night of her elopement with her first husband.

"Afterward, the man left her lying in a hotel. His mother showed up and offered my mother a mink coat to annul the marriage. My mother couldn't speak. So the man's mother, disgusted, brought her home to her uneducated parents. They had her institutionalized and got her electroshock treatments. She pretended to get well to get out of it. Still pretending to be well, she met and married my father to get out of her parents' house."

Liz was shocked and compassionate. "Wow. That's a lot of hurt."

"I know. My birth was a big surprise to her—she didn't know her body could work like that. That's why she never told me how my own worked—she didn't want to scare me with what she thought she knew. See, beyond surrendering my hymen, I'm afraid of losing my mind, too."

Kind Liz told me how lucky I was to have gentle Ernest interested in me. "Ernest would be the perfect guy for any girl's first time," she said.

But I didn't want to think of my hero as a merit badge for platoons of virgins.

"I don't want Ernest to be with just 'any girl,'" I quavered. "And I want Ernest to be more than just the first on some learning curve of men for me. He will be my first, and we will be each other's forever. He's very happy I have never had sex with anyone else."

Liz felt my icy judgment about others' promiscuity and commonness. Then I feared losing her ear and intelligence.

"But Liz? If I do say yes, I'm afraid of being bad at it and disappointing him. I'm scared to lose him either way—if I do it with him or if I don't," I told her.

Plus, I was terrified of getting pregnant before my acting career began. Liz recognized her limits and instantly retired as my adviser. She recommended that I get checked out by a professional, who could discuss my inhibitions and prescribe contraception, and gave me the name of her first gynecologist.

Making the trip from my college campus on Long Island all

the way to Brooklyn Heights on several trains to visit her doctor for the very first time, I was scared sick. I had never spoken to any grown-up about these matters before. I wanted fairy tale metaphors, not morbid details. But Liz had assured me that Dr. Irving Sugar was trained in all aspects of female sexuality. He had written books. I could throw all my extra aspects his way.

Ushered into his plush, red-velvet-furnished office, full of paintings of flower parts, bees, and butterflies, my floral skirt, high-necked blouse, and lace-up ankle boots fit right in. Taking on the role my costume and setting suggested, I spoke formally and objectively about every detail of my concerns to him, like I was describing someone else, removed from my conflicts. Dr. Irving Sugar nodded, and after I petered out, he invited me with an extended hand and a small, gallant bow into his examination room. His nurse handed me a soft cotton smock. Dr. Sugar helped me up on the table for the checkup in a courtly manner, as if we were getting in a boat to go on an evening sail, informing me kindly at each step what would transpire.

But he turned downright caddish when he brought his cold, harsh speculum to meet me and attempted to make the first such entry into my orifice. Not even I had gone in there. I had no interest in what lay beneath, as the outside of it all felt so great.

The instrument was spurned on its first four tries, but the doctor spoke to me gently, telling me to "Relax, dear, relax and push," as if I had control over the thing. Finally, I pressed down like on a tampon exit like Liz taught me, as he instructed on the fourth painful poke, then, with a deep, gauging push, Dr. Sugar ventured where no man had ever ventured before, and it hurt. I feared he had made a terrible mistake. My voice was shaky.

"Doctor? Am I still a virgin?"

He assured me that I was and helped me off the torture rack, inviting me to dress. Ho boy. If this was a harbinger of what intercourse might hold, I'd be far less inclined to ever recline with a member of this gender.

Sitting quaking in his office afterward, I was pronounced healthy, intact, and normal, except for irregular periods and the occasional pimple. Congenital defects would not provide me with any more excuses to wait.

"What should I do, Doctor?" I sniffled out all my fears about losing Ernest's interest if I gave in and then got pregnant, or if we separated for the summer before I secured his devotion. Dr. Sugar seemed flummoxed. I don't believe he had any specific answers for my overwrought queries, except to say that sex didn't always lead to pregnancy if one took precautions. Discussing precautions felt ickily out of range for the classic princess character in which I was trapped now, weeping.

Dr. Sugar began to write notations on a pad. I hoped he was writing Ernest a doctor's note, like *Fragile* or *Handle with Care*, or something. But it was a prescription for birth control pills, which were taken by most girls in my dorm. He gave me a box of my first month's dosage. He told me they would regulate my menstrual cycle, clear up my skin, and, most importantly, "keep your body infertile," as if that would retroactively clarify all the other matters on my mind about morality and permanence, and the trustworthiness of men and myself. He shook my hand in farewell, and his nurse gave me a card to remind me to return in six months.

Back to campus and to Ernest I went. I told him I was a normal woman inside and showed him the blister pack of the pills, like a small Swanson's TV dinner. We each licked the sickly sweetness of my first one, and I swallowed it like Alice in Wonderland beginning an adventure. He seemed as reluctant as I was to discuss the ramifications of the matter any more seriously than that. Wordy though I was, I couldn't find voice or vocabulary to express all my dreads, and maybe he couldn't, either. Without the right questions as keys, the answers remained locked inside us.

I recall how my breasts and behind began bloating up within weeks—"One pill makes you larger . . . ," I sang to myself—and my appearance mutated from innocent ingenue to va-va-voom voluptuous. I was fascinated. My skin cleared and my periods became regulated, but most significantly, I began to look like a woman, albeit a rather slutty one. Dr. Sugar's little pills had effects for which I had never prepared, as I bought briefer, big girl panties for my swelling behind and borrowed C cups to replace my Bs. I got cleavage. I filled out my slacks. Was this still me?

I could feel how my endocrine system was migrating into cahoots with Ernest's desires. My mind was tagging along like a druggy addict, as my stubborn virgin vote got outshouted. Getting pregnant could no longer be the excuse and the stopper. The attitude among most women my age, that the Pill facilitated, was "Hey, what the hell—why not?"

I didn't like how common my instincts were becoming as they skipped subliminal and social concerns. But I liked that my once efficient, hipless little walk had a womanly waggle. I liked how I looked in Liz-like pedal pushers and tighter tops. After all, sophomore year, I'd be leaving the classics and studying contemporary acting and improvisation. I felt my ability to play character roles enlarging exponentially, beyond my feminine soubrette/ingenue range.

People were noticing me—even professors looked at me askance—and looked less at my face, their eyes falling toward my chest and the rest. Like the white man in the hit book of the time, *Black Like Me*, who darkened the color of his skin and recorded how the world around him changed, I thought I'd pen a new book called *Breasts Like Mine*, about how people seeing me so differently made me act differently, in a continuous cycle of observation and reaction. Suddenly, my friendliness toward other girls' boyfriends was seen as flirtation and my dormmates trusted me less. As Liz seemed disinterested in mentoring me, her maternal nature now quelled, in the absence of any intimates, by further default, Ernest became my everything.

In June, Ernest took me home to Connecticut and met my parents and sister for the first time. They liked him very much, and I was proud. He and Daddy watched sports and ate Cheetos hand over fist, and he asked my sister about her artwork and she was charmed. Mom and I heated up a pot roast with potatoes Dad had made that morning, and I served it. All during dinner, my mother looked at Ernest approvingly and at me accusatorily, as if I'd pumped myself up to get a great guy and gotten happy, betraying our long alliance of resenting men.

That night, in a separate bed in my sister's room, I tossed and turned. Could I afford to wait? This night would be our last chance to touch for months. I had to do something to keep his interest. In the middle of the night, I snuck the few steps from her room into the guest room for our last nonstop hours of kisses. He held me to him as we wept in passionate anguish, coupled with uncoupled frustration.

As Ernest woke the next morning to my adoring gaze at 5:00 a.m., I boldly told him I'd give myself to him come September, were our feelings to remain the same. The power of my overblown body and my dread of losing him gave me moxie. More confidently than I felt, I looked into his beautiful brown eyes and said, "Can I touch you? Down there?" This was more as a science experiment than out of any zealous desire. His eyes widened, and it started swelling up just from my mentioning it. I felt I had some power.

Hard to believe this thing, for the first time fully exposed to my eye, was a part of Ernest. I'd always looked away, but now I regarded it in a friendly manner, put my hand carefully out to tame it. It reached to me, unafraid. He seemed to have no willful control over it—it moved up against gravity with no strings, no hands. Foreign though it looked and behaved, it felt as soft as a horse's velvet muzzle to my touch. I wished I could feed it something. Maybe this was the perfectly sized steed I'd been looking for. It seemed vulnerable in its fumbling blindness.

It grew and inspired my wonderment at its insistent pointing at me. I mustered some affection, called it "cute," but for this independent area of him I also felt sorry. I didn't find his erection any more relevant or attractive than I had pre-pill. Although I was bad at geometry and spatial relations, it seemed infeasible that it came in my size. I was still using junior tampons.

He had to be on the road by 6:00 a.m. so I made us tea, toast, and jam, and we tried to be upbeat. We walked out to his car, the air between us feeling so vast, I grabbed his hand in both of mine, admiring the bold little hairs sprouting vigorously from every finger. He put his suitcase in the little trunk of his car and turned, and we clung to each other.

"I really love you," Ernest said.

"I really, really love you, too," I said. So many of Shakespeare's parting words apropos to our anguish came to mind, but I could hardly speak. I let them and him go that morning with my heart heavy like a rock in my chest. I watched as his noisy Alfa Romeo revved, waved as it downshifted down my hill, waved as it turned a corner, listened as its engine Doppler-effected out of earshot as he drove north to a summer in Cape Cod and away from me, from us.

That long summer started with a lump in my throat, but it eased as I sang my way through two weeks of rehearsal and then two weeks playing Polly in *The Boy Friend*, then rehearsing to become Billie in *Babes in Arms* opposite the handsome John Drew Miglietta Jr.,—a nephew of John Barrymore, descendant of true theater royalty. I sent to and received from my Ernest illustrated love letters every day. We wrote poems and songs and circled our tearstains on the pages and our mouth-prints, too. We shared a talent for intense romance. I kissed his picture good night and good morning and often took a peek at his picture in the dressing room before curtain, showing him off to the girls in the chorus.

John B. Jr., Jr., my nickname for him that summer, and I got great reviews and pictures in the local papers for our leads in *Babes in Arms*. I mailed them to my mother and to Ernest, too much the show-off to consider the impact.

Mid-July Ernest's letters slackened to twice weekly, and I wrote him a letter one midnight that was twice as long as usual, then went to dinner the next night with John Jr., Jr. instead of with the other cast members. Ernest's next, impersonal letter came in the middle of the next week, with no tears or kisses circled, and I eased my anxiety by dining with John Jr., Jr. and his mother, Ethel Barrymore Colt, who flew into town in a small plane with her ancient oil magnate husband in tow. We ate at an expensive hotel, and I had filet mignon for the first time.

I wrote Ernest later that night to gossip about the evening

and wished ardently that he'd been there. He didn't answer the following week, or the next. I grew desperate to hear his voice, knowing something was wrong, if not with him then with our love. I wondered if I should call the next theater on his tour. As I rehearsed *Gypsy*, I practiced what I would say in my message to him all day. After several stutter starts, I actually called, but when the theater box office answered, I hung up, aflame with embarrassment. What if I pulled him from rehearsal? What if I seemed too needy? What if the director complained? He should call me first, I voted petulantly in my head. I would make him call with fervent, brow-furrowing wishes. But, much like when I wished hard, to the point of a headache, for a horse, nothing happened.

In August, I played Gypsy Rose Lee in *Gypsy*, and photos of me in fishnet stockings and a pushup-topped gown with long gloves were in all the syndicated Sunday papers in the Northeast. The show sold out every night. A New York agent and a talent manager came to see me backstage, but no interaction seemed as meaningful as mine inside my heart with Ernest. I couldn't see beyond my reunion with him toward a big Broadway career, and my throat bore a boulder of dread at what lay ahead. I returned to college for my sophomore year a nervous wreck.

Back at the dorm, there were no notes from him. I kept straining to hear his Alfa Romeo heading my way that first night to surprise me, but he didn't appear. I practiced how to behave when I saw him, if I saw him. The next day outside my sophomore Shakespeare section, I spied a familiar back in unfamiliar garb. A hippie guy with long black hair, Hercules sandals, and a peace sign on a T-shirt, who looked a little like Ernest if he were starring in *Hair*, turned to me, smoking a cigarette. He put it out on the pavement with his heel as I approached, stumbling at my last step.

"Is that you?" I asked, my heart in my throat.

"Sort of," he said. "How are you?"

"Fine," I lied.

There was a long, nontheatrical pause full of eye-averting and fascination with the butt still smoking on the ground. I summoned the guts to ask, "How was this summer?"

"Busy," he said, but he was still not looking at me.

We agreed he'd fetch me for a walk and talk on the beach that Saturday, and I didn't sleep the next two days. There had emerged a complex maze in the open channel that had flowed between us. How would we find our way to each other again? I asked more seasoned women in my dorm for advice.

He called for me at the dorm at noon on Saturday, and lots of nonchalant women were stationed around the lobby to look at him, spying for me or for themselves, I'm not sure which. I was still proprietarily proud to be seen with him, but now more possessive. As we pulled out of the parking lot in his noisy car, I wondered who he was now and what I was to him. He exuded marijuana out his skin and seemed a stranger I had never before kissed or touched. I clutched myself like I had chills, asking about his tour, getting grunts in exchange. My Ernest was trapped in there somewhere, and I was determined to get him out.

We walked barefoot in September sands, amid the still-blasting Indian summer heat. We strolled out of sync, without our hands ever gravitating to touch. He told me he'd had a few lines and a couple chorus roles in which, because he was strong, he had to lift the stars, but that he'd mostly done backstage work. My photo with John Barrymore Jr., Jr. had made him jealous, he said, partly because Jr., Jr. had his arm around me, but mostly because I was getting to play leads. I was getting lifted while he was lifting others. My heart plummeted into my belly. I imagined him imagining all the wrong things looking at the news clippings. What a dope I was.

"Then I learned that my number was near the top of the draft list."

"What? The draft?"

"Number 3 with no more deferments—my life is finished."

I felt ill. The Vietnam War was swooping so many guys out of their lives. Treating boys-in-progress like men. I had never considered the possibility of Ernest being drafted amid our drama department immersion in great plays and my many fantasies of us. We had never spoken about it. We had never spoken about so many other things. I couldn't form words to respond.

"Then, one night, when I was pulling the curtain for all the stars' curtain calls, Julie Newmar came up behind me and put her hands down my pants, and that was it."

It? TV's famous, sexy Catwoman? I wanted to throw up.

"And I was hers."

Hers?! I bottlenecked with images: her overpowering him and his surrender. She was so much taller, she could probably rest her breasts on his head. I was scalded with jealousy. I had lost a contest I never entered. The rarity of her beauty, her height, and her fame had trumped my one-of-a kind short package of virginity. The picture of him being hers or anyone else's made my eyes cross. The picture of my Ernest going overseas, fighting for principles he did not support, twisted my guts.

"And then when she left, there were others . . . "

He was destroying all hopes by telling me too much truth. The flimsy structure of trust we had erected toppled. So many hurts stockpiled, smeared together in a pool of paralysis. Sure, he must've been with other women before me. I never thought there would be any after me.

"Others . . . "

"First two, then three more, then three together," he said bluntly.

If he wanted to shock me off of him, he had succeeded. If he was slapping me for dining with John B. Jr. Jr., I felt it. If he was trying to let me down easy, he wasn't. My face felt frozen. I saw him fading across a widening sea of estrangement. I felt our attachment tearing with my heart. Our meant-to-be now meant nothing.

Still, underneath my hurt and anger, I felt sorry for him. He was no longer free like me and would have to drop out of college and all the now silly-seeming college plays. His summer of disappointment and lust had been an era of such uptick in my résumé and social standing. His priority was survival now.

"When will you have to go?"

"Pretty soon."

Sickened, I said, "Oh, Ernest . . . how I wish . . ."

"Hey, just call me Private Ernie now."

I couldn't. He wasn't. Private or Ernie. And without him, who was I? Like Cecily Cardew in Oscar Wilde's play, in which we had met and performed one year before, I felt the importance of him "being earnest." I knew this new being, Private Ernie, loose and loutish and unkempt, was not a man I could marry, even if he dressed and acted perfect as my hero again. He was too easily seduced into being other people and into being inside other people. Now he'd be a soldier, not my Ernest/Romeo, and I didn't know my lines for a new role opposite him.

He took me for my first banana split before he took me back to the campus. As he spoke of his summer and his altered life plans, like I was now his objective buddy, demoted from beloved, I remember eating the entire swamp of ice cream, whipped cream, broken peanuts, and chocolate sauce spoonful by mouthful. At the end of it, I remember trying to consume the unripe, too-dry banana, bite by bite. That was what having sex would have tasted like now. Beyond my capacity to swallow these new ideas, it stuck in my throat. And I watched his scoop of strawberry ice cream melt into soup in his bowl. He never touched it. He never touched me. And I would never touch him again. He raised accusatory eyes.

"I knew you couldn't really let me in. You were hanging on to that waiting till we got married bit as an excuse to get out of it."

"I don't know," I said, chilled by what he revealed about me to me.

"And I knew I might get drafted and couldn't ask you to have sex, then wait for me."

I looked sick.

"C'mon. We weren't gonna get married—you're eighteen, and you've got a big career already." Then, for the first time in my knowing him, his eyes grew reproachful. "But we could have given each other so much in the meantime if you had only trusted me. If you hadn't hung on so tight to that stupid myth."

Trusted him? Myth? We had barreled way past my asking what he meant by these complicated terms.

"We should have stopped kissing and talked."

"Yeah," he said, "I know. I didn't know how."

"Me, neither."

And now we were done, and he had brought me back to school, and I felt dead weight compressing my chest. His love had made me feel so good about myself, so grateful at feeling love at last. He showed me that being partners could be sweet, not like my parents' operatic tragedy of hate and hurt. His remove in this way left me loathing myself for how my delusions had hurt us both. Something was wrong with me. Playing romantic love, like in the movies, was the only love I knew.

The following Friday, I heard his unmistakable Alfa Romeo roar somewhere on the eastern side of the campus, no longer headed to my dorm, and it woke me. I snuck out of bed and ran in my robe and slippers across campus, noticing his red car parked at the graduate student dorm, now coed with no curfew. I was crazy to see and not to see, nor did I want to be seen, so I hid behind a hedge. Hearing two familiar voices, I spread the branches and watched now crew-cut Ernie and my ex-adviser Liz with her overnight bag, getting cozily into his car for a ride out to the beach.

My chest hardly contained a fist of pain as I hid, his headlamps scanning me. I'd probably have a heart attack like my father and be found dead in this hedge. The hurt went way past my ability to cry. I let go of the branch I'd been clutching so hard I bled and fled back to my dorm.

The flimsy structures and hopes that had secured me toppled. I buried myself in studies of drama, directing, and improvisation those next three years, as first the Kent State killings, then the SDS sit-ins and protests of the war in Vietnam decimated the normalcy of college life. The relationships between authorities and students, much like the sexual mores of the times, disintegrated in a Zeitgeist of change.

Ernest left for basic training without ever reaching out to me again, but he lingered in my dreams and self-reproachment for years. I would think of him with every lesser man I met or kissed. I obsessed about him, driving myself nuts going through all the possible permutations of what might have been had I gone all the way into love with him.

A no-frills graduation belched my still-virgin self out into the wider world with a BA in liberal arts. I knew lots about acting, but nothing about living. I took on the mantle of grown-up but felt far from it. My body was filled with sorrow, and it took me a year to even look at my body or touch myself again. I definitely had to postpone involving another person in my pursuit of pleasure for a long, long time.

FRUGGING FOR SHAKESPEARE

I was only fourteen when I got discovered. Sixteen-year-old Shauna Weisman saw me doing the Mashed Potato at a sock hop and mirrored me move for move.

Shauna was a blonde Jewish American Barbie Doll with a Mustang, a big allowance, and no curfew—all the advantages of a broken home. As I mimicked her grooves, she asked me, "Hey. How would you like to do a go-go dance with me for two hours at a sweet sixteen this weekend? I would give you a third of what they pay me, which is ninety dollars. I can set the whole thing up with the girl's mother."

She was a seasoned wheeler-dealer and I had no questions. I was thrilled and said I'd have to ask my parents. She shrugged and said sure. She'd outgrown having to ask her parents anything long ago.

We watched *American Bandstand*, *Shindig!*, and *Hullabaloo* and made up a whole routine, adding in great moves the groovy local Black boys gave us when we danced together, mastering the Monkey, the Slop, the Twist, and the Bristol Stomp. She gave me her old pair of scuffed white go-go boots, loaned me a sailor dress. With her platinum pixie and my brown ponytail, we were a great team. As usual, my mother said it would be up to my father.

"Over my dead body," Daddy groused. "No daughter of mine—"

"But I'll make thirty dollars for just two hours—much more than babysitting!" I cajoled. He thought deeply for an instant. "Be home by eleven, dear," he revised.

Phil Spector watched the two of us dancing at a Bar Mitzvah the following month and hired us for even more money the following Friday. He was managing Black girl groups like the Crystals and the Ronettes and figured us wholesome high school white girls could help them cross over to a wider, whiter audience. We did great and adored those women.

Within a year, Shauna and I were shakin' it in cages in clubs and at Yale mixers, getting ogled with lots of "R-E-S-P-E-C-T" from cute Ivy League guys. The crowds and money got bigger, the rooms draftier, and our skirts shorter and skimpier, but our exhibitionism kept us warm. We had a great ride until I retired to study theater arts and especially Shakespeare at a small private college on Long Island. How I loved his multifaceted plays—highfalutin lovely language and low comedy characters. I felt the possibility of that whole range in myself, too. I wanted to feel it all.

After three and a half years there, I was fed up with my course of studies learning speech therapy and drama history from tenured dilettantes. Our only acting teacher was an alcoholic, and when she didn't show up for morning classes, and Shakespeare fell off the curriculum, a classmate, Donald Wollner—like me a rabid fan of Mike Nichols's and Elaine May's improvised albums—took over class with me, and we taught theater games from a book, *Improvisation for the Theatre* by Viola Spolin. We taught what we needed to learn.

I loved Viola's emphasis on flexibility of voice and body, on adaptability to other players, on conjuring stories together. I loved the dance of collaboration in the moment with others. I intuited this would be an important skillset in my arsenal, not only for work, but for life. The heads of this drama department weren't preparing us for an acting career. They were preparing us for fallback jobs as failed artists, none of which I wanted. They disbelieved any of us could make a living as actors, just like my father did.

So, as a college senior, bored and broke, I read up on job opportunities in *Backstage* magazine and saw one that might suit. On the spot, I decided to make my go-go comeback. Dancing to funky soul music had so far made me more money and kept me more flexible than acting in Molière. And it was far more fun than forcing speech therapy on lateral lispers.

So, one Friday I carried my overnight bag of dance outfits on the Long Island Railroad into New York City. I hiked up a crooked, creaky staircase into the Phil Franco Dance Agency.

The cigar smoke was so thick in the outer office, I could hardly make out the pictures of tassel twirlers and belly dancers yellowing on the walls.

"Somebody out there?"

"Hello, Mr. Franco? I'm the dancer? I have an appointment."

"C'mon in."

A wizened little man behind a desk, holding a phone and a stogie, gestured to me to sit.

"What can I say . . . the dame got sick," he said as he checked me out. "Who the hell knows, cramps, a cough . . . she can't make it. Okay? Substitute? What? In two hours? I can't line anybody up that fast. Oh yeah? Ah, screw you, too!" He slammed the phone down.

"How do you do, Mr. Franco? I'm the dancer from—"

"Had go-go experience?" He squinted at me through cigar smoke.

"Well, yes. I danced at Yale, at a double sweet sixteen, and I study jazz dance at college."

"You free for a job tonight? Pays forty dollars an hour—three-hour minimum. One-night guarantee to start. I take 10 percent and tips. Gotta call the guy now. My word is your bond."

"Okay!"

He scribbled a booking slip and dialed simultaneously.

"Now you're very wholesome. I would want to preserve that."

"Oh, me, too . . . "

"Morty? Darling? You're in luck. Gotcha a girl. Seven o'clock she's there. Treat her nice . . . college kid, okay?" He shoved the paper at me. "So here's whatcha do . . . You go to Port Authority right down Eighth Avenue here, take the 5:05 bus to Passaic, NJ. Ask the driver to drop you at the bowling alley. Ya climb over the esplanade, call this number from the pay phone in dere, and they'll quick come pick y'up."

"Oh, thank you . . . I'll do a good job, I promise."

An agent and a job on the first try? Feeling spunky, I bussed and climbed and clambered and called, and a wise guy in a souped-up Caddie fetched me. He drove me to Morty's, a large truck stop diner/bar/pool hall off the New Jersey Turnpike. It was so dark inside I could hardly see the bartender.

"Hello. I'm the dancer. Where's the dressing room, please?"

He pointed down a darkened hall.

"Dressing room? We got the one john—down there."

Urinals have always nauseated me, especially with those blue scent dispensers staining the inside, making an overstink in a small space. I stepped into my sailor frock and white boots for my first dance set in years. I knew it was all in me and would come back to me fast. The bartender shoved my bag under the register. I looked around the dimness and asked what time the band would arrive. "Band? No band. Here's nickels. Pick your tunes on the jukebox, climb up on the bar, and do your thing."

How degrading. Failing to find any Motown, which always got me in touch with the soul I assimilated from my Black dancer buddies, I chose from the meager selections, then struggled onto the too-narrow bar. Every pair of eyes aimed toward me as "The Lion Sleeps Tonight" pumped out of the tinny speakers. I began moving to the beat, hoping against hope that I'd get in a mood. But as customers turned back to their burgers and beer, I felt very alone up there.

I couldn't locate my cool to "Hang On Sloopy." It wasn't available in a room devoid of atmosphere, amplifiers, or interest from the customers. Shauna's steps weren't going to work here, and my half of the Hully Gully could catapult me into little glasses of onions, olives, and slices of lemons and limes.

"I Want to Hold Your Hand"—I couldn't find a feel, so I pantomimed the words with my hands.

Then "The Lion Sleeps Tonight" again—oh, this was going to be a looong night.

Ten lousy songs later, I was running Portia's "The Quality of Mercy" speech from *The Merchant of Venice* in my mind, perkily swaying as an older man in a summer suit came in, ordered a whisky sour, and sat at my feet swirling it, smiling up at me. Finally. An audience. I'd use the suit man to awaken my muse's moves.

But then, "Hey, bitch . . . I'd sure like to poke in those tights. Show us what you got, ya little pussy. Want something to eat? Bite my dick burger—nice and rare. Comes with soup!"

Guffaws were building. He now had a bigger audience than I did.

Blech! Indignant, I climbed down and huffed over to the bartender: "Please ask that man to leave."

"Uh, sorry. No."

"Well, make him stop. I've never been spoken to this way."

"Hey, what you want me to do . . . that's Morty. He's the owner—ten years. You been here two hours. Why don't I just give us all a break and bounce you instead."

"I can't go! I have a contract."

"I'll get you a lift right now to the bowling alley."

"Please! I've never left a job early or been fired from anything in my life. What would Mr. Franco say? This is our first agreement, and I have to honor it . . . "

"Okay, okay. Suit yourself . . . You're done at ten, though."

I flop-sweated as Morty's inebriation and imagination intensified, and his white man audience howled. Ick. Men were vile and repulsive animals. Eyes on the prize, I was determined to survive it for my own edification, like how building the pyramids made the Jews stronger.

Sniffling in the stinky bathroom on a break, I noticed a sign on the wall, itemizing the fire law limits, naming the proprietor: Morty Weisman. It rang a bell.

As I struggled to dance to "Volaré," he started in again.

"Hey, little pussy. Nice *pulkes* ya got there. Why don'cha take off that fuckin' outfit and dance on this?"

I yelled back at him over the lump in my throat, and the whole place went quiet: "Excuse me, sir. Are you Shauna Weisman's father?"

Putting down his drink, he sobered up a little. The truckers looked up from amid their burgers and beers, as the juke music ran out.

"You mean Shauna from New Haven?"

"Yes," I said easily above the sudden hush.

"She's my niece. My brother's kid." He sneered at some jeering around him.

"She's a very nice girl—very good dancer, too."

"Uh-huh. Why? You her friend?"

"From high school. We did some nice dance jobs together. I'll call and tell her we met."

"Do me a big favor," he snarled. "Don't."

Mortified Morty slunk away a few minutes later, leaving a five-dollar bill at my feet. I ignored it.

I force-fed the crowd the Hully Gully and the Popeye until my awful night ended. Eyes avoided me as I called the guy to drive me to the bus.

My brand of go-go had gone-gone, degenerated into dirty dancing while I was oblivious to the outside world, struggling to evolve as an actress.

Shakespeare and Molière had endured for ages. I would, too.

AN EMPTY SPACE

A s I was retiring as the arts critic for my college paper, it was arranged for me to review British director Peter Brook's hit production of Shakespeare's *A Midsummer Night's Dream* on Broadway. Thrilled, I pledged I would get an interview with the renowned author of *The Empty Space*, every word of which I'd sucked through my eyeballs into my soul during directing courses in college.

I was delirious with possibility, puffed up with importance. Now that I was moving up in the world to live in squalor in Greenwich Village, this could be my first foothold to play with players on the Great White Way.

With a crowd unified in joy, I inhaled the innovative production, performed in a bare white box under bright light, the actors dressed like playful hippie clowns on trapezes and stilts, carnal in their enactment of the besotted lovers. The language was spare, pure Shakespeare, without pretentions or pomp. Lights and wires and technicians were exposed, yet our suspended disbelief was willingly thrown like roses at the stage.

We all rose as one at the end, applauding until our hands numbed to stumps, and I strode outside to the stage door, flashing my college press pass to the stage manager. I was struggling to form sentences to describe the novelty, magic, and pure impact of the performance in my review. I began wording pithy questions for Brook, preplanning the eloquence with which I'd deliver them, the vocabulary with which I'd impress him, to let him know I was not just some kid off the streets.

I introduced myself in my big girl voice with a few theater-savvy compliments to the handsome, hairy Ben Kingsley, the lover Demetrius in *Midsummer*, the first to come down the stairs. Excited to make contact with anyone who was part of the phenomenon, I told him I was there to interview Peter for my college paper. He smiled and said the cast was on their way downtown to a party with Peter and I should join them. He and Terence Taplin, Lysander in the play, invited me and my awe into a yellow checker cab. We sped south of my new stomping grounds in Greenwich Village, inebriated by the sheer exhilaration of being associated with the hit of the century, on our way to see the toast of many towns. I was exhilarated just being in a cab.

We took a freight elevator up in what seemed to be a factory building. I'd never seen the gears and pulleys that make lifts lift. New feelings, new possibilities were brimming in my brain. I was about to sneak behind the scenes to mingle with creators of sublime theatricality.

The doors opened, and I followed the boys through a beaded curtain into a large, dark loft, spotlighted in moody hues of purple and red, smoky with incense. Someone played sitar, another played a big didgeridoo in a corner. About thirty artistic types were engrossed in intense conversations around the vast space. I was in Bohemia and loving it.

Diminutive but Protean Peter was sitting on a tuffet at a large round table holding court with admirers lying around him on a Persian rug. Judith Malina and Julian Beck, masterminds of the anarchist Living Theatre, welcomed me to sit by them at the table and offered me hashish from a hookah. People at this level of legend loved turning on eager naïfs like me, as we were so portable and impressionable. I partook of a small amount, praying to coalesce with them into cool, as I was very susceptible to intoxicants and already flying high as helium. I listened to others speak, trying to sneak peeks into the esoteric, to understand the clockworks of the glory they innovated.

Kingsley introduced me to everyone at the table as a cub reporter, the new company mascot, and as Peter aimed his piercing blue eyes into me, all my fancy-schmancy words and pre-rehearsed questions left me. In his calming eyes, I felt his gift for transcendence, for rising above the mundane, his command of the profoundly simple. I knew that despite his small stature he contained enormous power.

At that moment, I felt he truly saw me, and I was curious to know what he saw, wanted some hint of the truest path for my huge hopes. Then, my pot-induced paranoia kicked in, and I felt guilty for monopolizing so many seconds of his attention. Choking up at his sincere interest all I could muster was a reverent "Thank you."

He received it as if I was important, me, a nobody of zilch accomplishment in the arts, but full of raw desire for connection and creation. And he seemed to tear up with me. And in stillness, we shared a red-rimmed moment of truth, a giving and receiving of recognition in a mere moment of wordless attunement. If only I could imagine my life from inside this glorious empty space, free of the negative point of view that was my family heritage, shorn of the "I'll show 'em" drive that kept me so off-balance, I could maybe make some of my crazy dreams realities.

In his exquisite attention, I felt inducted and empowered. It was far more important for me to get that story that night than to capture any interview.

FANHANDLING

The Vietnam War raged on and on, and boys just bristling into manhood with big dreams were getting drafted right out of school against all their principles, parking all their personal wants for a future they hoped to see. Our government was ruthlessly taking the lives of the Vietnamese and eating its own young in equal measure.

These were desperate times. My best friend and improv playmate Donald, voted least likely to ever be a soldier, enrolled in the National Guard just in the nick of time, as his draft number was up three days later. So rather than go to the warfront, he'd go into basic training for many months with the army at Fort Campbell in Kentucky. This backup Army Reserve was very unlikely to be tapped for any combat.

I couldn't imagine this nice Jewish wordsmith intellectual crawling in mud, carrying firearms anywhere. Denied contact of any kind with the outside world, his chummy phone calls to me ceased. I missed our talks and laughter terribly as I started a hardscrabble life in New York City. I was determined not to lose another man to the war in Nam and insisted on being in touch.

Between typing jobs, I got a small recurring role on a soap opera, ABC-TV's *All My Children*. Now my mother and father could see me captured inside the box inside their house, where I never wished to live again.

"They did your hair so much better on the show," said my mother. "Why can't you always wear it like that? Even your father said he liked it."

My father took photos whenever I was on the TV screen. These images would be my effigy, my proof, for whenever they missed me or stopped believing in me.

On the show, I played Sally, a freshman working her way through college in the cafeteria. I was befriended by a senior played by handsome Richard Hatch, at the time the hottest daytime television star in the business.

He was getting more fan mail than he could handle and offered me a job answering it for him. He'd sign a few hundred postcards graced with his face in advance, but wanted each fan to have a personal message, as if penned by him. He'd pay me by the pound. Sure, I said. I wrote a few samples pretending to be him, and he felt I captured his sincerity to a T.

He supplied me with stamps, and we weighed many sacks of mail. For weeks I worked part-time in his apartment, far larger than my tiny flat. I read every single piece, fascinated by the power a supernova in the subculture of soaps had over hearts and minds. I read messages from many a lovelorn groupie, old and young, female and male, who said he was the light of their days. It was gratifying to give these lonelies some joy so easily. I'd even answer their thank-you notes for the autographed pictures, with a few generous words, unless they seemed a bit too delirious about being answered or got demanding, at which point I'd stop responding. I always felt badly about letting anyone down.

One day I recognized a return address. A thick multipage letter sent from the military base at Fort Campbell, Kentucky, where my friend Donald was stationed. Poor Penelope was thirteen and very lonely living at her colonel father's house, and she poured painful, candid feelings out to Richard Hatch. Just knowing he was reading her words made her feel better, she said.

Now here was a multipurpose ghostwriting opportunity. I responded fully, thanking her from the bottom of his heart for her words, telling her that a favorite old friend and scene partner, Private Donald Wollner, was stationed in basic at her father's camp. Perhaps she might enjoy having a conversation with him sometime soon. I sent it out like a message in a bottle cast to sea and then forgot all about it.

A year later, when Donald was sprung from full-time army maneuvers, now only needing to report to his platoon as a weekend warrior to maintain his status, we reunited for a happy catch up. He told me he had barely survived basic and was thankful it was over. Then he related an unfathomable incident that occurred one afternoon as he was lighting up and smoking a joint behind the rifle range.

A master sergeant and his driver pulled up to the range in a Jeep, asking the commanding officer for the location of a Private Donald Wollner. Hearing his name bandied about, Donald tossed the joint, pretended to be taking a leak behind the target, and struggled to get his stoned wits about him. The two solemn men, guns holstered on their hips, approached. Donald resheathed himself.

"Will you come with us, Private Wollner?" The sergeant asked.

Donald was unnerved, fearing he'd been caught red-handed, not just with his penis out, but with the discarded pot. He was about to be court-martialed or declared AWOL or shipped out to

Nam, and he was in no condition to talk his way out of it. He kept his chattering teeth clenched and mouth shut for the ten-minute ride. Without any explanation, he was driven to a large private home on the outskirts of the base. He was marched up to an imperious front door, the bell was rung for him, and a plump little teenage girl dressed up in a lovely frock introduced herself as Penelope and welcomed him happily inside.

She served him tea and cookies and asked him many questions about Richard Hatch, his scene partner. At first Donald thought he was hallucinating, but, scraping out his foggy brainstem, he managed to improvise tales of many experiences he'd had as an actor coming up in the ranks with Richard, of whom he had heard but did not know from whence. And with a bad case of the munchies, he devoured many a cookie as Penelope kept him talking for about an hour. Then she walked him back to the Jeep for his ride with his military escort to what had become his now-normal life of playing war games.

I told him I'd puppeteered this whole incident under my nom de plume, Richard Hatch, and we laughed and laughed. And then we hypothesized with horror how badly things might have gone. Prison for Donald? Obsessive madness for Penelope? Plus, I could have lost this cushy ghostwriting job, this fun of imagining myself in the role of a handsome hunk, embodying the noblesse oblige of the famous giving token thrills to subjects. Despite loving the power I wielded in this win-win, I knew I'd been playing with fire. If I were ever a celebrity, I would be kind and very, very careful not to lead folks on.

From then on, I avoided giving any instructions to the fans beyond "Thank you, and please keep watching."

ROAD TO THE STARS

Tuesday noon at last. I typed up crew expenses from the Clark chewing gum spots. I asked my boss one extra time extra-sweet if he needed anything, just for cover, and he waved me off with a wink and twinkle. I snatched my purse and portfolio and snuck out of the office for a long lunch hour, away from account executives and art directors, away from the world of commercial production, away from my worries about survival in a tough town, and ran as if unhinged for the crosstown bus.

Heart pounding from more than the physical exertion, I jumped off at Forty-Second and Eighth Avenue, stepped over a drunk sunning himself on the sidewalk, and averted my eyes from the businessmen ducking into peep shows near Times Square. I felt like an adulteress unfaithful to my day job.

I dashed to the address given, a doorway next to a porn movie theater, and flew up slanted stairs, dented deep from a million tap shoes. I passed through a narrow hallway, drenched in the stench of folks striving beyond physical limits for their art, and joined a long lineup outside a large rehearsal studio. So many triple threats here—singer-dancer-actors trying out for a "top secret" new Broadway musical. Their warmup hums created an overture of excitement. Their stretching legs formed a Rockettes-worthy kickline as I excuse-me'd my way to sign in. I changed to my dance shoes. They were running late. My turn wouldn't happen for an hour. Good—I needed the time to map out how I'd deliver. Bad—now I'd only have an hour to audition, then flee back to work for a 2:00 p.m. meeting. Hell with that. It was my turn to sing, to sweat, to shine, to pursue my shameful secret life.

On the bus back I reviewed. I'd sight-read a snazzy song, cold-read a sonnet, improvised a scene, moved to strange choreography. They applauded. Were they that nice to everybody? They asked if I could start Friday. I said sure. Oh, yeah sure. It would make a big problem if they hired me, but wouldn't it be utterly glorious to be on Broadway? I made them laugh. They tested my range vocally, physically, asked if I could trampoline. I exaggerated a big, "Oh, yes." Now I had to let it all go, diminish my way back to my day job—make calls, type forms, arrange our next shoot, behind the scenes, behind the camera, behind the curve ball as a production assistant instead of in front of the curtain as an actor.

I allowed myself one free call from the office at the end of each eight-hour day to my service—Plaza 3-2310. My heart elevated—no messages—then dove. Okay, so maybe they hadn't decided yet. Maybe everybody was so great it was hard to choose. Maybe I was just kidding myself. Maybe continuing this $160 a week job, with the possibility of promotion to producer and a clear, predictable path, would be the wisest life move. Maybe my father would be happy. Maybe I could sleep tonight. Maybe I could stop replaying it all in my mind as I dragged myself home to my fourth-floor walk-up apartment in the Village.

I got through the next morning. And the next. *Don't cry yet.* If it hurt to hope, to give up would hurt horribly. Friday morning, I found it a drudgery to move the cover off the typewriter, to brush out the crumbs of Wite-Out from the typos I'd made on every page. I hefted the receiver of the lit-up phone.

"EUE/Screen Gems. Mike Elliot's office."

"I've got good news," said my agent, the only one who had this number for emergencies.

"Charles?" This was an emergency.

"Congratulations," he said. "Your first Broadway show, and it's a big one."

"Oh, oh, great!" My eyes misted, then dried. "What do I have to do? Where do I have to go?"

"Rehearses two weeks at the Ukrainian Home downtown—you play a blue Earthling in act 1, a green Ithacan geologist in act 2. Galt MacDermot, composer. Peter Hall of the Royal Shakespeare Company, director. Broadway scale, $234 a week, plus $15 for singing, $15 for dancing, $15 for special business, and an extra $20 a week for a split-second nude love scene on a trampoline with Raul Julia"—I loved Raul Julia!—"but it's covered with a light change and you're painted blue, so no one will notice."

It was a fortune, but my exhilaration screeched to a halt as it sunk in. "Hold it. What?" Kissing Raul Julia would be thrilling, but naked scared me on many levels.

"I can get you more than that—maybe fifty dollars for the nudity. Or not . . ."

It wasn't a matter of price. Something in my soul knew to say, "No. No. I can't do that. I won't do that. I'm sorry," like a big girl with principles.

"All right, I'll tell them," he said, resigned. "May make a difference, but we'll see."

I wanted to be taken seriously. I wanted to do classics. I wanted a long career. Not to be a thing, not for my parents to see me like that. Diane Keaton didn't take her clothes off for *Hair*, and things were going pretty good for her.

"Wait. Wait! Ask them if I can maybe wear a blue body stocking. Paint on or glue on the private parts—then they could make them much bigger if they wanted to."

"Like a tight nylon stocking, with falsies? Okay. If that makes a difference to you."

To have something between my skin and their eyes? Between me and a man? It did.

"Can't have my father or my friends see me naked. Even if they can't tell the difference, I'd know the difference."

"I'll tell them no nudity," he said. "Good luck to us." He clicked off.

There were probably a hundred other triple threats with dancer-perfect bodies who would bounce on a trampoline naked for twenty dollars a week with Raoul and be thankful. But I was newly deflowered, new to the big city, new to a career, and scared. The pull to be held and, more, by a heartthrob of a man was so powerful that I'd need as many membranes as possible between me and temptation. I wasn't yet sure what my body was for, as I couldn't foresee marriage and motherhood pending anytime soon. I just knew it wasn't right for that.

I prayed for the first time in my life. Called up to a cinematic cumulus cloud in the sky over the Hudson River through the window of the Tenth Avenue office. Imagined the love I once felt with my back sitting up against my late grandma's bosom, her arms wrapped around me in her lap. Then I prayed to an imaginary Jewish God/Goddess because She/He seemed much more *hamish* and showbizzy than all other gods, much more of a New Yorker. I named my god Sydney, as a Sydney could be male or female.

"So, Syd? Sorry for not calling sooner, for not meeting you in the temple like truly good Jews do. But the theater feels like my place of worship. Having faith, believing in a pretend story with a bunch of other believers, feels like a religion to me, and I hope you can show up in that world because, after all, you are omnipotent, more than any fairy godmother in the sky or genie in the lantern. Hey, by the way, I wish that *Jesus Christ Superstar* had celebrated Christ's Judaism, instead of having the Jews portrayed as smarmy villains. I promise that I will create a good Jewish geologist in the new musical, if you'll just put in a good word with the producers, who are probably Jewish, too.

"And while I have your ear, how about a little protection, forgiveness, understanding of my choices that my parents couldn't give me? So I won't feel so alone, like I'm floating loose in space. Please give me courage to face the intimidating things I'll encounter on my path."

No answer, but then I felt something shift inside me that maybe was always there, or maybe I made it up. A fallback, a certainty, a trust crept in out of nowhere, like I'd never felt with my anxious parents. Something was on my side. As an actor, I already knew how powerful belief could be, that it could change you from the inside out. I was determined to believe in this belief.

A quiet morning at the office. Too quiet. Two hours later, I picked up the phone on the first half ring.

"Can you get there by noon?"

"Did they agree?"

"Crazy lucky—yes. I got you twenty dollars extra for the exposure in the body stocking and falsies, another thirty for hazard pay. It's 120 Second Avenue. We'll work out the other particulars, the length of the contract, and my 10 percent later."

I didn't know what hazard pay meant, but the naked hazard

was gone. I didn't want to ruffle many more feathers. "Hey, what's the name of the show?"

"It's called *Via Galactica—Road to the Stars*. It's a space-age, science fiction rock opera, first of its kind with a great pedigree of presenters and players, English groundbreakers and American theater innovators. Good luck. You're in a whole new world now."

I was, and even if Sydney was just a placebo, imagining His/Her benevolence gave me new confidence.

Now to tell my boss, the great Mike Elliot, winner of many awards for Best Commercial, my favorite the one of the Indian chief weeping at the sight of trash on the shore of the Hudson. Mike was bigger-than-life, an artisan of this art form—the sixty-second story. I was so fortunate to look through the lens of his camera, to be told I had a future there, but I was now about to toss him and this job right out the window to be a nice Jewish geologist in a Broadway show.

I knocked on his office doorjamb—the door was always open.

"Yeah," he said.

"Mike, you know how great this job is."

"Yeah," he said.

"But you know my first love is acting, and I just got my first Broadway show."

"Good for you," he said. "Now make some calls. Order me tuna on toasted rye. Then call the Alka-Seltzer client. Tell them if they want those two giant fizzy tablets built to bubble, we'll be way the hell over budget—"

"You don't understand. I have to go. I have to go right now."

He was seasoned. He was wise. He didn't miss a beat. But he didn't twinkle.

"Call my daughter," he said. "She's taking a travel year off from school, so tell her she needs to help me out before she goes."

I knew that paternalistic tone too well—some other daughter would be surrendering her wishes to her father's will. I felt awful that I would be cause, messenger, and beneficiary of his command. "Then you can leave," said Mike. "Good-bye, good luck." I smelled a bridge burning. "Okay," I said. "I'm sorry. You've been great."

He was on so fast to the next thing, it hurt. For him I was history. But for me I was future.

I left a message with his daughter's service, grateful I wouldn't have to hear her response. My darling deity put an arm around me and helped me gather my hidden résumés, scoop my headshots from the bottom drawer of the desirable desk where I'd spent the month, and put them into my big bag. Helped me walk out the door and board the crosstown bus, then transfer to the Second Avenue bus down to the Ukrainian Home. Why was I a different person on this bus than on all other buses? Because I now had a nice Jewish god buddy and I was Broadway bound, about to show my folks I could turn a dream into a career.

I joined a group of thirty actors of all ages, races, and types, all percolating with excitement. As we arranged ourselves into folding chairs before a full-size mock-up of the set, leather-bound scripts were bestowed on us like Bibles. Peter Hall, founder of Britain's Royal Shakespeare Company, stood upon it like a colossus encircled by a team of choreographers, designers, and their assorted assistants.

Jimmy and Jackie, seated to my left and right, both seasoned Broadway performers I'd seen around town, introduced themselves, as did Mark behind me. I cast a shy glance past them toward Raul Julia. He allotted me one warm smile, his glasses barely dimming the wattage of his appeal. Damn. Some people are so attractive that you feel seduced and reduced just by proximity. His eyes resembled my first love's, the man I'd lost first to other lovers, then to the Vietnam War. They reminded me of the vacuum inside me, hungry to suck someone in.

Peter strode to the stage edge, and, already cowed by his reputation, we whooped in expectancy of being wowed by whatever the hell he had to say. He made serious eye contact with each and every one and began to speak in stentorian tones.

"Welcome and thank you all for joining our journey to the stars, a most groundbreaking adventure, with each of you an essential, invaluable element in embodying this cautionary tale. Let me describe the technical wonderments we will present in the brand-new, state-of-the-art Uris Theatre."

He gestured grandly to miniaturized set pieces and sample attire on a nearby table.

"Earth has become ruler of a vast empire of many planets in our constellation, governing with an iron fist. In the first scene, you inbred Blue Earthlings will each wear one of these gyroscope spinning hats to control your emotions, as ordained by an invisible Earth Power."

I needed one that very moment, as nerves, hopes, and fears clogged my brainstem. He gestured to the elevated wooden stage inset with three circular trampolines.

"During the next scenes, most of you will make quick changes into other colors and become hat-free escapee rebels on the remote, low-gravity planet called Ithaca at the edge of the galaxy. These trampolines will be camouflaged as craters, from which you will leap as though weightless to traverse it."

My brain went weightless trying to fathom all this.

"Raul Julia will embody the fable of Gabriel, a blue garbage-man looking to rid Earth of its trash in the outer realms of space, as nearby planets have been polluted beyond salvation. He'll make a grand entrance in this space truck."

He held up a blue model that seemed a futuristic version of a rocket-powered antique car "It will enter over the audience, drop from the rafters over the orchestra, and be lasered onto Ithaca. There Gabriel will be enticed to take off his blue control hat and mate with your golden queen, Omaha. This kidnapping and seduction is orchestrated by your own Dr. Isaacs, Omaha's ancient sterile husband, reduced to naught but an overdeveloped brain. Dr. Isaacs will be operated from offstage in robot form on hidden tracks. And the education of Gabriel to the Ithacan credo, and his courtship by your queen, will be facilitated by all of you. Questions?"

I looked to my left, to Jimmy, and to my right, to Jackie, seeing the same strain to comprehend in their eyes as I felt in my own. We were too stupefied, afraid of looking unintelligent, to form questions. Raul lilted in his Puerto Rican accent, "Ummm, wellll?" which allowed us all to laugh a little.

But I understood this much: old-fashioned soubrette, student of Stella Adler and the classics, I was to be part of a revolution in modern Broadway musical theater. The radical poor man's theater production, *Hair*, free of sets and sometimes costumes, had hit it big downtown, then up, beyond all expectations. *Jesus Christ Superstar*'s unconventional concept-album-to-hit-production sequence was a milestone. The unconventional new musical *Dude*, for which the venerable Broadway Theatre had been gutted, rebuilt, and strewn with sand, was about to open to big buzz. Our science fiction rock opera, all sung, not spoken, opening soon in a brand-new Broadway house, would be the most revolutionary yet. Fare thee well, *Oklahoma*. Auf Wiedersehen, *Cabaret*. I was about to embark on a new road to the stars.

Calling us to arms, Peter proclaimed, "All right, then. You Earthlings and Ithacans, let's begin," and we cheered.

For eight weeks, we studied movement with masters and music with maestros. We learned to catapult up off the trampolines and dance in midair and sing Christopher Gore's poetic lyrics to Galt MacDermot's catchy tunes toward the many microphones suspended above us. We laughed and napped together, cuddling like puppies in the trampolines, becoming a bonded family like I'd only found in theater. We lost touch with the real world as we entered twelve-hour days, spending nights barely recovering to start again each morning. It was as though we were stranded on an island, receiving no bottled messages, never seeing another shore. And just like desperate escapees to an isolated planet, we became attached to each other's voices, bodies, and talents, and to eating Sardi's half-price lunches, a privilege of Broadway actors.

As preview week approached, technological snafus proliferated. Mark sprained an ankle and Jackie got mercury poisoning from her shiny silver body makeup and was replaced by an understudy in a duller gray hue. Gabriel's garbageman belt got hooked into my blue body stocking, tearing it open during our timed quick-change, joining us at the pelvis as Raul's fiancée hovered nearby. Gabriel's spaceship got snagged in the rafters, which took hours to remedy, and the Dr. Isaacs robot slipped some gears. We began to talk among ourselves at a Sardi's supper.

I divulged that the blue body paint and yellow spray paint intended to turn me green for my Jewish geologist role had stained my ears and underarms. Others grumbled about their feet and costumes catching at the edge of the craters as they leaped in keeping with the ever-changing choreography. The emphasis on clever tricks and Dadaisms started to feel like a smokescreen created by the Wizard of Oz, and all felt that the production and lyrics were too complex for the simple love story it intended to tell. Basically, a liberated woman teaches an inhibited man how to be free and fall in love. Together they journey with us rebels to create new life in a brave new world.

With no explanatory lines of dialogue, the audience would have to extrapolate the tale from the poetry set to music and the subtext of our interpretations, like a classical opera, only in English without a libretto. We hoped we'd get the message of the story heard above the style.

We returned after supper to our last full technical and full-dress run-through before our first preview for the public the next night. Tensions were high. A number of backers and producers and press people were assembled to watch, as were musicians and synthesizer guys, who would make space-age sounds to underscore our lives. Tonight, we'd perform the finale with full orchestrations, full effects, all the rigging, all hands on deck, all systems go.

The stage manager called us to Peter's opening pep talk, and our leader paced before us with a furrowed, fervent face.

"Long have you toiled, much you have accomplished, and our journey is just now about to begin. Make us all believe in each and every one of you creatures of Ithaca. Tell this beautiful tale of freedom from your hearts. And as you say here in the USA, break a leg."

We mustered applause, dispersing to be colored, coifed, and costumed. I tried to check in with my God buddy, but She/He was drowned out by the contagion of raw nerves and zeal.

All was smooth sailing as we hit our marks, found our lights, and sang our songs. The backers and musicians in the pit were rapt, new to all our phenomena, and cheered us on. The orchestrations were thrilling. Hey, I thought, maybe this thing would overcome the odds and fly. We summoned our reserves for the big finish.

As ordained by Dr. Isaacs's robot head, we Ithacans had built a three-stage spaceship to flee Earth's search party, which was barreling toward us to retrieve Gabriel and his garbage truck. Fearing being found and inbred to be a blue race again, we rebels would climb the skeletal fire escape staircase. Our narrator, Irene Cara, added to make the story clearer, would sing the refrain to Galt's gorgeous anthem, "New Jerusalem Will Rise." The stairs would rise into the tail of the enormous mother ship resting over a crater as we sang. A deafening 85 decibel roar in quadrophonic sound, with smoke jetting from the tail, would conclude our stay on Ithaca and the show as we headed for new galaxies far, far away and big profits for years to come. I was counting up my weeks of salary so far—it was more than I'd earned on all my acting jobs put together since I'd embarked on this dream.

The cast, with our orange youngest member, Ralph Carter, boarding first, climbed the staircase, singing heralds to celestial universes yet to be known. And, as planned, we began to rise up into the ship. Some dust fell on me, and I thought some new effect was being tested. We all heard a creaking sound above the roar of the orchestra and explosive effects, but, directed to sing the last modulating chorus out to the audience, no one looked up. Then our ascension jerked to a stop. The entire staircase swayed, dropped to a slant. Time stood still.

In slow motion we began to descend, jerking left and right, as scraping, destructive sounds that were not preplanned overpowered the orchestra. I heard screams from friends at the bottom, screeches from little Ralph at the top, yelps from orchestra members hit by flying debris, and bellows from the wealthy backers in the audience. I was screaming, too.

But part of me stayed clear, and as I awaited death's impact, I saw my résumé pass before my eyes. Not my real life. My fake life. I was speed-recalling all my little credits, concluding, *At least I made it to Broadway.*

In crisis—in the actions you take, the words you say, the thoughts you think—your character gets revealed. I realized an acting career meant more to me than life itself. I cared far more about pretending than being, about characters I played more than myself.

And we fell, cables snapping, metal whining as the staircase with us all aboard smashed through a trampoline into the bowels of the Uris Theatre, and all went black.

I was bathed in a shaft of white light. I opened my eyes. Stage lights were pouring through the gash in the trampoline above. I was apparently alive because my hands hurt from white-knuckling the aluminum banister. I reached for a moaning purple Ithacan sister, her leg going the wrong way, and yelled for help. Crew dove in to lift the staircase off those at the bottom, to carefully check us all for blood and breakage.

Ambulances and medics arrived to take the injured to the hospital. Aside from bruised palms and heels, I was pronounced okay, but many of us left in pain and shock that night. The remaining company mutinied, without getting our customary production notes from Peter. We all walked out and called our agents.

"Nobody's taking responsibility," Charles told me the next

morning. "Act of God, they're saying."

Speculation was that the winches had pulled loose from the reinforced concrete ceiling of the new theater—that the designer's calculations about our combined weight had been inaccurate. Charles told me that, in accepting hazard pay, and in having no serious injuries, I was legally contracted to go on with the show, and not to disclose the nature of our accident. That secret was hard for any of us or the press to keep.

And after a brief delay the show would go on, despite evidence to the contrary. Most of us in small parts were told the same: take it and go on, or leave it, in breach of our contracts.

The Broadway theater had proven very heartless and inhumane in this, my first show. My acquired family, our remaining company of actors, asked Actors' Equity to make demands: Reformulate the body paint. Sand down the fake lava. And all equipment was to be tested before each show by the producers or crew, and not by us.

Our diplomatic huckster leader, Peter, plus doubled hazard pay, encouraged us to come back a week later. His soliloquy, delivered as the crew and producers themselves mounted the well-hung staircase to demonstrate its safety as it rose, was the performance of the season.

"We assure you that the equipment will forevermore be triply tested before each performance." He dug in for the from-the-heart part. "Now, you have rehearsed for months, you've given your time, voices, blood, sweat, and tears to this newest planet in the Broadway constellation, to the most revolutionary work of art in the canon of modern musical theater. Great art takes great risk, and you've put yourselves at that risk. Yes, a few comrades have been felled in the struggle, but you mustn't stop now. You must go on, complete this work, for yourselves and for your eager audience, to set an example of courage for the world, just as the Ithacans would do for the future of humankind in the universe." No one clapped. But after a time, Raul, who was earning three times as much we did, said in his affable way, "Okaaay. I'll go on." Then, twenty of the most dedicated/desperate of us opted to go on, too, taking the singing lines and harmonies of the fallen, like vultures circling carrion. I certainly didn't feel courageous. I was frightened, not just of all the machinery and daring the show required, but because this musical felt like all I had in the world to live for. If the show didn't go on, I might not, either.

In ten more days of previews, choreography would change during the day, and forgetting it one night, I got run over by the robot. I added a cane to my characterization. I wanted to buy back my invitations to friends and family to come to our grand opening night, which felt like doomsday. Nonetheless there was deafening applause at show's end. To us it felt like pity applause.

My parents waited out front, looking very foreign to me. What planet were they from? Theater gypsies/warriors were now my real family. I had never seen my parents this dressed up—my father in his Johnny Carson brand plaid sports jacket from Sears, my mother in a new Sears polyester pantsuit. Having heard about the supposedly hush-hushed accident through my sister, who was studying scene design in college and in on the grapevine of crew gossip, their anxiety about her and me was palpable. My mother was scared.

"You looked like a little doll up there on that big stage dwarfed by all that machinery," she said. "Please be careful."

"This isn't like the little kid school plays, you know," snarled my father. "You and your sister could get killed in a place like this. It's your fault she followed you into doing theater. I want you both to get out of it right away."

The time was not right for a fight, so I hastily excused myself for the low-key opening-night party, where the company, clinging to one another, steeled itself for the reviews. There was scant praise for the talents involved, and the book and the production were hammered hard.

As we read the closing notice on our third and final night, I was despondent about losing a job and my first New York City community of people who joyously flexed their talents and making money, many of us first-timers on the Great White Way. I said stinging good-byes to the supportive crew. I felt deeply bonded to my new brothers of color, Mark and Jimmy. We had survived an experience that would be hard to explain to anyone. We all said we'd stay in touch, but as this failure cast a pall over us, we dispersed in our separate disappointments, exiled to seek livelihoods and companionship by other means. My heart ached.

Taking my very last bus ride as a Broadway actor to new digs I'd rented uptown with rash optimism, just forty-two steps from Broadway, I was crushed. So I tuned deep inside to see if my nice Jewish God friend would stick with me.

"Sydney, oh wise one of show business, I can't tell if you saved me or forsook me and let me nearly die like everybody else. Were you teaching me a lesson like my father would—'You'd better get a real job, kid.' Was that message about having no real life a warning from you?"

A wise, patient silence ensued. Typical.

"Give me a hint—if I'm not on Broadway, if I'm not to be an actor, if I'm to be a regular boring ordinary nothing of a person, will you still be with me?" I asked.

I listened hard, squeezing my brain like a sponge to make room for new moisture.

And I thought I heard something say, "If you listen, if you believe in yourself, wherever you are, I will be there."

EXTRA CRISPY

tried out along with lots of others and got it—my first regional commercial. I would get a session fee for the shoot and residuals for May through September. And if it tested well enough regionally, my agent would renegotiate a bigger fee for subsequent runs. I felt good. Being chosen was great, and with dollar signs attached all the better.

I was just beginning a career in television after years working in the trenches in off-off-Broadway theater with little recompense. I was getting more recurring roles on soap operas, getting inside people's TV sets where more could see me in their homes than in some old off-Broadway theater. In this thirty-second Schlitz spot, the male voiceover would say: "Barbara was my sweetheart that summer of '62. Well, I lost the girl, but I've still got the beer. Schlitz—the beer that made Milwaukee famous."

The storyboard depicted a guy and girl sitting on a beach blanket picnicking near the ocean on the first page. On the second page, they clinked beer cans in one frame, sipped in another, enjoyed the beer in another, and then kissed in three frames—a long kiss. This nostalgic scenario would be shot as if it were a home movie, with sepia tones, static and jump cutting. I'd be silent, playing the old-fashioned girl that the boy liked.

I was relieved that I wouldn't have to be the pitchwoman and promote a product I never used or liked. I wouldn't have to tell anybody I never drank beer. I hadn't yet told my agents that I wouldn't be the spokesperson for products I wouldn't personally use. At the start of a career, I sensed it would be best for business if I didn't assert too many principles.

When they told us to dress extra warm, it hadn't occurred to me that we would be filming at Jones Beach in bathing suits in early March. They drove ponytailed me and the guy playing the guy in our overcoats and gloves from Manhattan at 8:00 a.m. toward the sea. In the trailer at the beach, they put us in our old-fashioned bathing suit costumes—mine blue gingham with a flouncy little skirt, his modest plaid trunks. The makeup lady put tan body paint on every visible inch of us to promote that golden summer feel. I loved my tan, even though it was fake. It was a goal I had never attained in real life when I'd been slathered with baby oil and iodine at my local beach. I could never lie still long enough to tan.

The guy playing the guy was named Martin, and I tried hard not to notice how cute he was, with soulful brown eyes and a thick mane of black hair. But he was smiling at me all the time, and it was hard not to smile back. We stayed in the heated trailer as they rehearsed and lit with stand-ins. We chatted about our careers so far. Not much to discuss, but we enjoyed talking. Then we were called to make the long trek across the sand. Jones Beach was enormous, accommodating millions of sun lovers each summer, but it was empty now, except for our crew.

They took off our coats, and we sat on the beach blanket. Even in the hot lights, the sand was icy hard and the wind chill made it worse, but we didn't complain. Actors, I thought, needed to be stoic and never complain about conditions that the crew was enduring, too, especially since we were making more money. After the third rehearsal, film rolled, and we clinked and sipped and kissed deeply. And often. We got good at it real fast. I thought we were done at noon, but then it was time to move the enormous camera to different angles, each of which took twenty minutes or more to set up. It was too far to trudge back to the trailer, so they gave us our coats. When they weren't enough to warm us, the crew threw soundproofing quilts over us, too.

Between his close-ups and my close-ups and shots of the waves crashing as we kissed, I was turning blue, so they put more rouge on me, which made me ghoulish, so they redid my whole face. Finally, they wrapped big blankets around Martin and me, and he warmed me skin to skin, full frontal, saying it was his professional duty to keep me comfortable. We also liked it. A lot.

I tried not to notice how nicely he was built and how perfectly his chest hair sprouted out, how warm he was, and how hard he was getting. I'd only recently been deflowered but knew enough to know when someone was attracted to me. All the creature comforting we'd done with each other made me more attracted to him with every three-frame kiss and warming hug. My skin felt sunburned, like I was hot for him, and my body was blushing. *Maybe I'll marry this man*, I thought. *He's nice.* Judging from the Polaroids the assistant had taken, we'd look good together as we aged.

At 4:00 p.m., we wrapped and dressed, and Martin and I were covered in blankets for the darkening trip in traffic back to Manhattan. We stayed cozy and close all the way, even on the wide back seat. It turned out he lived near me and all the great take-out spots at Seventy-Second and Broadway. Amazing how millions of strangers inhabited these little nooks we called homes within a stone's throw of each other, without knowing each other in the crowded city. As we staggered out of the car, he asked if he might treat me to Kentucky Fried, extra crispy. He'd done a national commercial for it and wanted to be loyal.

I invited him to share the greasy feast in my modest, high-ceilinged apartment, so much bigger heightwise than it was lengthwise I wished I could turn it sideways. I put down a blanket, and we continued our picnic on my parlor floor. Eating with our hands, we finally felt warm and were finding more and more to talk about.

I asked if I might take off my makeup. He offered to help. I meant face, but we stood in my tub, and he rubbed me very gently, as my skin had gotten scorched on my shoulders and nose. Then, with permission, he peeled off my sandy gingham suit, then he asked if I might help him clean up, too. We felt natural as could be. We laughed as our tans washed into orange puddles in the tub. My skin beneath where my suit had been was winter white with freckles. His was beautifully clear and, beneath his suit, ivory. We already knew the feel of each other's bodies well, but we were discovering brand-new things now in our nakedness.

I got bold and asked if I might let down my ponytail because my scalp hurt, and he said, "Please do."

And my hair fell below my shoulders, and as he touched it gently, he asked, "Now, would you mind if I take off my hair?"

"Pardon?"

"My hair," he said again. "See, this is a hairpiece, and my head itches from the glue."

I honestly wanted to shout no, because it felt far too soon for me to see him this way. Never might be better. Even though I had already viewed him with his clothes off, this was a kind of naked for which I was not prepared. But one of my newly forming principles was to be kind rather than cruel. I didn't want to hurt the feelings of this lovely person, who until seconds ago I thought I might marry.

So, I heard myself say a weak "Sure."

And he slowly detached not only his thick black hair, but the entire top of his well-shaped head. He took it off and put it in the sink, revealing a skull paler than his chest and flatter than a pancake in the back.

I suppressed my horror. I was an actress, and this was good practice, I rationalized. He pulled the gumlike glue off a forehead that now went all the way to the nape of his neck and continued with no breaks and down his back to his butt. I feared he might remove his chest and arm hair, too, but apparently that was all his.

"Now, may I kiss you in real life?"

"Um . . ."

"I know I may look different, but I am the same man," he said gently.

"No, you most certainly are *not!*" I snapped inside, my newly forming principle of truth-telling duking it out with my manners. I'd invited him inside my apartment but was wary of letting this polite imposter inside any more things.

This Martin seemed a far different Martin than the one who'd held me confidently under the blankets and kissed me in front of the cameras. That Martin was virile. That Martin might have been a Martin I'd introduce to my mother. That Martin had been an illusion with a toupee. Now I had gone so far that it felt unethical to stop, impolite to renege, hurtful to reveal my dismay. His treating me to extra crispy, my invitation upstairs, and his hard-on seemed irrevocable. As a teenager, I'd heard women being accused of causing blue balls, and now I felt pressure to comply so men wouldn't suffer that excruciating pain I would never know. Better I suffer unwelcome penetration as punishment for being a tease by dint of feeling sexily attracted to a myth in my mind.

I couldn't recover from my shock and bewilderment with manners sufficient to form a decisive no or a fake yes. So, I decided to close my eyes, picture the guy in the commercial, and dive into the illusion of Martin. I would do the wrong, immoral thing, for the right or kind reason. But my fantasy heart was no longer in it.

Afterward, I asked if we could please be just friends in the future.

I lost the guy, but I still got the residuals.

GREEKS BEARING GIFTS

We got comfortable together doing a musical comedy re-vue at the Motel on the Mountain in the foothills of the Catskills, or the "Kittenskills" as we five called them.

It was non-union, but fun, steady, easy money for starving artists still waiting in the wings of their big dreams. As a serious student of Stella Adler, and the newest to sketch comedy, I learned to play full-out, face-making, over-the-top farce, ad-libbing, even talking back to hecklers. Sometimes I'd stoop so low as to break down weeping to guilt-trip the smartasses.

"Look what you've done. I hope you're happy, showing off to all your friends, ruining a girl's moment in the sun." I'd run off sobbing crocodile tears.

Let It All Hang Out had three shows every Saturday night, and all shows sold out—the 6:00 p.m. supper, the 9:30 p.m. drink-er, and the 11:30 p.m. drugger performances—with audiences growing more raucous and hysterical as the hour grew later. We drove up and back every Saturday and stayed sober, but the mo-tel guests could get falling-down wasted to the point of puking between the tables and wheeled in luggage-carts to their rooms.

All sorts of lovers came to see us: singles, marrieds, adulter-ers, even some ménage-à-trois types away from New York for the night. "Where the elite meet to sneak" was our nickname for the place. One night a lovely couple invited me for an après show drink at Swingers bar and to stay over that night in their suite so I could walk with them in the mountains the next morning. Such a sweet offer, I thought, longing to roll in autumn leaves on the hillsides, until my castmate Crazy George pulled me over and explained what Swingers was meant for.

We funny-boned five would enact every off-color joke in the book, sing racy, silly songs, many of which we wrote. George, older and more seasoned than the rest of us, was a first-generation Greek American from a gang of eleven funny, competitive big brothers. They'd had a baby sister, he said, but she had fallen or maybe jumped out a fourth-floor window at age three.

He had mastered low comedy to survive in his family, he said, then got cast in Chicago's Second City improv company. This guy had great comic chops. He'd improvise walk-ons in wigs, hats, and noses to pull the shows together. He had a trunk full of tricks—he'd balance a champagne glass glued to a beret on his head as he crossed the stage, impersonate Harpo with a bicycle horn, and leer at the ladies while strolling the aisles in drag wearing fishnets and a red boa, smoking a Tiparillo crushed into the cigarette holder gritted tight in his teeth. This guy was funny on the fly. He loved to chase me around the stage honking, and gave me notes on tapping into my vulnerability, helping my bits be more potent in their subtlety.

We five laughed a lot on our two-hour ride back to the city. As the smallest and youngest at twenty-four, I was usually stuck in back, in the middle between George and hilarious Debby, feet up on the hump. I'd listen to all the wonderful talk and start nodding off as 2:00 a.m. drew a curtain across my brain. After resisting for a few weeks, I began to let myself get pulled onto George's shoulder for the trip home. In a couple months, I became aware that he was whispering muted messages in my ear, telling the others he was hypnotizing me.

"You're going to love me. And you're going to marry me, little dolly. We're gonna get a big place uptown together. And you're going to give me lots of babies that look just like you and me."

I'd giggle him off and doze deeper, but I was getting lulled as the subliminal messages began to become liminal. Men have sneaky ways of getting you hooked, and I was too susceptible.

He was complimentary and avuncular, and, although educational—which moistened my mind—older, which dried me up like a drop of water on a frypan. As I got dropped off first, he'd walk me to my building door, give me a big bear hug, then walk a few blocks to his home. I let the hugs get a little longer as months of Saturdays wore on. His age seemed to diminish as months sped by, as he got more youthfully happy being near me.

We pulled out all the stops when our last show finally staggered to a finale, with the three guys mooning the audience, smiley faces drawn on their butts. I knew with this ending I'd feel more alone in the world, and I clung to the last dregs of the tight-knit clique we'd become.

We all stopped for a celebratory drink and big hugs in town, and only George stayed sober, walked me home at 3:30 a.m., walked me upstairs, walked me inside, and walked me into my first grown-up Greek man kiss. It lasted a nonstop hour. It ended when I ushered him quickly out, but it was warm beyond all imagining.

Then the full-court press of courtship began in earnest. He invited me out to a formal dinner at his club the following Friday, the Upstairs at the Downstairs, where he was the big shot weeknight host and general cutup, introducing comedy revues with

Fannie Flagg, Lily Tomlin, and Joan Rivers.

"You could do that," he said, "but prettier."

I thought I maybe might. He said to put together ten minutes and some characters, and he'd direct it and put me on. I was grateful for the possibility. Feeling his advantage, he asked if I'd come up and see his place, then he'd walk me home. Just for a minute, I said, hardly stepping in the door. His apartment was full of memorabilia from his long career—lovely art, rugs, posters, and great books about spirituality and theater, his favorite topics. I stepped further inside to see things, smelling stale pot blurred by potpourri. Big mistake. He had to show me his pièce de résistance—his big antique brass bed. I admired the bedposts, the shine. He invited me to lie on it. I said maybe some other time and scooted right home alone.

I was wary. He was reckless and needy for his age, and sad behind his clown cover. I didn't think I could reciprocate his very obvious affections, but agreed to sup with him at the club again and sing at the Downstairs bar so he could show me off to his boss. It could be a big break.

As soon as he saw me enter the club that night, he began performing for the drinking crowd. He jumped on the bar like a chimp, aping all the customers, just as Irving, the old grouch owner, came in.

"Hey, you! This is the last straw," Irving yelled. "I gave you three chances, George. Now get off the damn bar, get all your stuff, get the hell out and never come back!"

Sick at heart and humiliated, George packed his trunk of tricks, and I, sunk at heart and sorry for him, walked with him as he dollied them the twenty blocks home.

As we got out of his elevator, we saw his lock had been picked and his door was ajar. Aghast, he had me hang back. He shoved the door open with karate arms on alert, shouted a warning, and entered. No one answered back. He flipped curtains and opened closets, cursing. I stepped inside. His apartment had been ransacked, his pillows tossed around, his art strewn across the floor. It was clearly not just money someone wanted. This seemed a personal assault on him and the things he loved.

The home he'd lived in for years now a crime scene, he was disconsolate. I asked him who his enemies were; he said he had none, but he couldn't bear to be in his flat like that. I told him to call the police, and with the pity I'd feel for any good friend, I said he could stay on my couch for the night as he pulled himself together.

He parked on my couch a few nights, then on the couch of another of his friends. He said he was searching for a new apartment, then began making presents to me of his personal belongings. First, a book he loved. Then a vase I liked. Then a marble-topped end table I'd admired. A man starts giving you his best stuff, it means he plans to move in with it. He gets access to both of you, I learned.

It was getting far too cozy on winter nights with him around. He was fun and such a good cook, if sloppy. His avgolemono soup was spectacular, his lamb chops with feta succulent. He cooked like a man used to eleven brothers, strewing dried oregano around my tiny kitchen till it crackled underfoot like autumn leaves. And he was so creative. One night, as I was plunking away on my upright, playing and singing a new song, he lifted and took me right up on the keyboards, as the ivories crashed beneath me in an avant-garde accompaniment.

He was my third lover ever, and it was a crazy ride as he

parked his trunk of tricks in my pad. Underneath the funny noses and glasses, there were handcuffs, a bullwhip, and all kinds of getups for all sorts of kinky scenarios in his arsenal—and proposed literary ones as well. I'd be Lady Chatterley; he'd be the gardener. I read and turned down the lead in the *Story of O*. But still, so imaginative, I thought. I often told him I did not love him despite being fond and attracted and grateful for his mentoring. He'd just smile, and I'd surrender. I'd close my eyes and try to bury my lost college love in this man's body.

I didn't mean to let him move in, but I gave him a key so he could come and go. One night when I came home from a temp typing job, he'd made me a present of his beautiful brass bed, and he was on it, playing a ukulele, crooning like Bob Dylan warbling "Lay Lady Lay"

Everything he did sounded silly to me, and I laughed and laughed. I'd had my mattress on the floor, so he put mine on top of his and offered me a mounting stool he had brought from his place, inviting me to climb on. I did and stayed rigid. Soon he pulled me onto him and lulled me into a sensuous sleep. I liked feeling this loved, lying on his hirsute chest, listening to his big heart pounding.

In the morning, over his freshly served spinach omelet with melted feta, I froze up. I told him I didn't want him giving me more stuff or staying over anymore, and he countered with the same proposals he'd murmured under his breath in the car, this time melodramatically on one knee. I chortled. I found everything he said hilarious. He laughed along, but he knew I knew he meant business, as he lured me into another erotic spell. Even in the grogginess of lust, and the laughing aftermath, I knew I'd be nutty to get serious with him.

At one point I wondered if I was being set up. Had he had some wise guy friend savage his apartment to make me feel sorry for him, to get my sympathy if not my love?

Nah. Nobody could be that desperate, I assured myself—as desperate as me.

So, I drew up a one-month roommates' agreement. We would split the rent and the household chores. We would sleep on separate mattresses, one on the floor in the parlor, one on the brass bed, our togetherness being negotiated each night, our contract being reevaluated each month.

Six months into our cohabitation, my agents arranged for me to go on at New York's Improv Club the night George Schlatter, star-maker of Goldie Hawn and Lily Tomlin, would be scouting talent for the new *Laugh-In*. I'd cobbled together some special material, songs I'd written, which I sang in offbeat characters, with patter between. On the big night, I was singing a demented love song about falling in love with a man's feet, when my crazy Greek roommate flapped up in clown shoes, ever the improviser, and tried to take over my act. Flop sweat was beading on my brow as I tried to joke him off, but he hung on like a laugh-mad bulldog. We struggled for an excruciating few seconds, then I surrendered as if it was planned, and stormed off in an oversize theatrical huff to cover my mortification.

I should have seen it coming.

He had been slipping over the edge from comical pothead to paranoid problem child, his perceptions of reality growing more and more askew. Just weeks before, he had made me a gift of Al Hirschfeld's caricature of Woody Allen, which he'd stolen from Sardi's. Priceless. He seemed surprised I wasn't grateful.

"Are you insane?!" I hollered. "Do you know how valuable

this is—what trouble I'd be in if somebody saw it here?"

"You're worth it, baby," he crooned to me.

He was losing all sense of proportion, but I kept postponing the inevitable rip apart a breakup would cause. I knew I'd feel beyond alone in a George-less vacuum.

Over the next weeks, I'd see debonair Jack Rollins, Woody Allen's personal manager, on the 104 bus going down Broadway at 9:30 a.m. Every few days I'd make up an excuse to go downtown and creep nearer to him with Woody hidden in my portfolio, pretending I had no idea who he was, trying to figure out how the hell to slip it into his briefcase. Or to maybe be more direct.

"Excuse me, Mr. Rollins, I'm a fledging comic. I couldn't help noticing you—I've seen you at the clubs—and I have something in my possession that just might interest you. And if it does, would you perhaps consider signing me?"

Then I'd whip out the framed piece.

And then any further conversation would be halted, and I'd probably end up in jail. I tried to figure out who the hell in my world of stand-up guys I could bribe to slip it back onto the wall of Sardi's main dining room, without getting anybody or myself implicated.

Weeks later, a friend from the Improv Club signed with Jack Rollins. I told him what I had and how bad it could go for me if I was implicated. He took it in a brown paper bag one day and told me he'd say he found it in a trash can and simply hand it back directly. No problem. Crisis averted.

I should have seen it coming—how small irritations could ulcerate into disasters.

George had taken to spraying Streaks 'n Tips colored hair spray on his thinning hair, giving his scalp and my white tiled bathroom a dark-brown sheen, and giving me a phlegmy cough. He'd begun checking most nights when I got home to make sure my bra hook was fastened to the same loop as it had been when I left for the club. One morning he took two of my long hairs from the tub drain and secretly hung them across the handle and just inside the drawer where I kept condoms to make sure it wasn't opened during his days away. He flipped out when it was gone that night, disbelieving that I'd opened it to get my ChapStick. He had nightmares that I was shtupping all the comics at the clubs. No amount of defending myself seemed to appease him. He wanted much more than I could offer, and I was scraping the bottom of my patience with him. But I needed the rent money. And I liked the love.

■

The bewildered crowd eked out a stingy smattering of applause as I stepped out of the room to face the music. George forced a few minutes on the crowd before owner/emcee Budd Friedman led him off and out. My agent intercepted me and said, "George Schlatter wants to talk to you. This could be good, kid."

I ducked into the restroom, trying to rise above a cesspool of shame, nerves, and hope, pinched my cheeks, fluffed my hair, scooped and lifted out my breasts to cleave together in their cups, like that might make some big difference. I approached Schlatter at the bar.

"Lovely to meet you." I think I may have curtsied—that's how unused to big shots asking to meet I was.

"Pull up a stool," he said. "You've got some talent."

"Thank you," I said.

"Lotta training?"

"Yes—singing, acting, dance, improv . . . "

"It shows. Look, can I give you some advice?" he asked, hefting an expressive eyebrow.

"Yes. Please."

"That your boyfriend?" He gestured with his chin to George, who was currently causing a kerfuffle in the hall between the bar and the main room.

"Oh. Yes," I mumbled. "He is."

Schlatter repositioned both brows deep down into his eyeballs and leaned in. At a blurry close range, I recognized this as a scowl.

"Get rid of him," he said, direct, emphatic, deep into the pit of my ambition. He nodded me off the stool of honor. "Good luck."

I staggered away, knock-kneed.

My agents were on me like flies on carrion, wanting to know what he'd said. I kept it to myself. This was not career advice. This was weighty life advice from a man who'd climbed up the ranks and made it big and who could maybe see my future obstructed, could see the albatross hanging around my neck. Something was very wrong with this picture.

Much as it felt good for me to be loved by someone, by anyone, the funny guy squatting in my apartment did not coexist with my dreams for myself.

THE TROJAN HORSE

I boarded the crosstown bus and transferred to the uptown local in heavy traffic, trying to outrace it as it journeyed further inside me, taking up residence, seeking custody of my will, my organs, to make them its mother.

"You're not using all this," the growing zygote says. "Why can't I?"

It's the second thing I want to scrape from my body.

"I'm not loaning you money to pay your Actors' Equity dues, not buying you any audition shirt. I'm not letting you live here anymore, even if you do pay me the back rent. I'm sick of your promises and lies. I don't love you. It is *over*."

He had finally heard me, knew that I meant it. I let him in one last time to pick up his things, resolved not to laugh at this silly guy who I'd been loved by so much. He handed me a check, to pay what he owed me these last few quarrelsome months, and the key. Good. Then he crept into my lap and wept.

When a funny man is sad, it's the saddest thing of all. I gave him time, gave him an "it's over" cheek kiss and pat. He kissed an "it's still on" deep past my lips. I kissed off "no." His tears continued to flow, wetting my breasts, my dress, my belly. I held him, pangs of pity moistening me, as he named and kissed my parts good-bye one by one, and then I was crying, too.

He had seduced me with his unique brand of hilarity. Distracted me from my underfunded, overtalented determination to study the craft of acting so I could be truly good, so I could make a living. He had mentored my stand-up act, taught me great tricks. And then he became my third lover since being deflowered, my two-year teacher of all my body could do, who satisfied curiosities it could hardly contain.

He said he would be the only source, that no one would ever love me like him. He pulled the crotch of my underpants aside this very last time to pleasure me, as he so often had, like nobody ever had before. I closed my eyes to receive his tongue's fervent parting gift, his last love words and touches. I knew I would not let myself get this close to a man for a very long time. I knew how great the risks. I lay in a moment outside of time, in that altered somnambulist spell he always created. And feeling my vulnerability, he pulled a bait and switch, entered, and his cum came in waves delivered deep before I could pull him out or off or even knew it was happening. I yell.

"No, no! Stop! You can't!"

He did. He had.

Pinned flat by his weight, I feel the ping of life in a place I'd never felt a thing before. Something lit a flame in a room that had never seen light before. A guitar chord twanged, echoed off a wall that had never heard sound before. Some dormant part of my womanhood was waking up.

I thought, *Fuck! I am fucked!*

He knew damn well I was off the Pill for health reasons, and that my heightened fertility had become my chastity belt, a warning, a no-trespassing notice as he moved his things out of my life. My fertility would thwart my craving, my addiction to his silliness—his big seduction for me. Laughter was miswired to create crazy lust in me. Fear of pregnancy lost me my sense of humor.

"Why did you do that?" I screamed, panicking in his crush of captivity, scrambling, bucking the fucker off. He gripped my hips to keep me still.

"I love you, baby. I want to marry you. Nobody will ever love you like I do. I want you for my wife forever. You're gonna have my babies. You know that's what's supposed to happen. You know I'll make you safe."

Safe? Getting safe from him was my frenzy. Rearing up, I snarled, my voice new to me.

"I don't want you! In any way. I told you over and over and over it's over. Now—get out!"

Good thing I didn't have a gun. I'd never been this mad, even when teen me was pinned by a stranger with sexual assault in his eyes. I'd never seen it before, but I sure recognized it then. My smartass mouth talked my way out of that, but it couldn't talk my way out of this. Inside someplace, this already felt irreversible.

"My *kukla mou*, my little dolly, you know I'm the one, the best man you ever had—the best you'll ever have."

Now I saw he was not the funny, gifted Greek man I thought for a long while I loved. He was not the talented genius everybody said he was. He was not headed for stardom and success. He was crazy and had just been proven dangerous.

He collapsed on the couch in a stoned, smug sleep. I drank big gulps of water and tried to pee him out. Who could I call for help? Actors' Equity? Not the police. They'd think I was pretty stupid for letting a crazy man live in my apartment, and they'd be right. The only other tough guys I knew were his friends, and most of them flirted with me behind his back, and he'd accuse me of provoking them like a little *poutána*.

·

All the traffic lights are blinking red. Traffic is honking go. Power outage, someone says. I look at my nailbeds—blue, like my lips, for weeks. I've had a migraine since the first moment, a 60hz hum in my head, as I feel this unwanted thing growing, grabbing for its supplies, securing its claim on life. It wants me. Like he wanted me. For its own good, not mine.

Get me out of here. Get it out of me.

As the bus creeps uptown, I pull the get-off cord, and as it heaves to a stop, I fling out the back door twenty feet from the curb. I'm running in my oldest overcoat, scarf, and sneakers, not dressed to impress, dressed to repress, to hide my body's mistake. I'm sweating. People are honking, yelling. It took me eight long, scary weeks to earn this money at typing jobs, my body hidden at big desks. Now it's running for its life. Near to fainting, I come to a halt in front of the new Women's Free Clinic—to me a church of salvation. I sprint in.

"I have a 10:00 a.m. appointment," I pant to the receptionist.

"We're having a power outage," she says. "A brownout. We've got the generator on, but I'm not sure it's enough to operate the machinery. There'll be a delay in all procedures today."

"But I have to . . . I am not leaving this building. I need to see someone now. I have to get out of this, get this out of me as fast as possible."

Harried, she takes a call. *Take a number,* her eyes say, just like at the deli. She gestures to chairs containing other worried women, younger and older. I sign in last on the page on the clipboard.

I plant a chair and sit in front of her. Squatters' rights. Abortion is finally legal now, here. It is my right. I know I'm lucky, even in the midst of my unluck. She can't stop me. Outages can't stop me. I will not budge until this baby is out of me.

No, not yet a baby—this thing. I can't personalize, can't think about its feelings. I must call it "it." We haven't met. It doesn't know me yet. It doesn't know my face or voice. It can't blame me. I did not invite its life. He did. We were forced together like a blind date, mismatched by an enemy in an arranged rape. *Oh no, I called us "we." Stop it. Tell it—it's got the wrong girl. Sorry. Maybe another time, another life, another man, another me, baby, maybe.*

For a half hour I grip the armrests until my hands tingle, until the Valium kicks in. Then a motor starts running outside the building, and a few lights flicker on in the reception area. A nurse comes in, in an overcoat. I can see her breath. She confers with the receptionist. She approaches me with the clipboard.

"Hi. We're delayed. Just need to tell you, you might want to come back another day when we have heat."

"No," I grit through chattering teeth. "This has to happen today, please."

"All right, but," she whispers, "there'll be no amenities. Keep your coat on. It's cold in there, and much noisier than usual— equipment's running on a generator." There was care in her eyes.

"That's okay," I snivel in grateful response. As long as it drowns out the noise in my head, in my belly, his begging and blaming in my ear, I don't mind. She beckons another woman in for an exam. Then another nurse beckons someone else. The whites of my eyes are showing, I'm sure. Every minute on its way to a heartbeat accelerates my panic.

At last another nurse brings me into a room, lays me on an exam table, helps pull off my bottoms, puts my feet in stirrups, covers me in my coat with a blanket. It's too dim to read the plaques and licenses framed on the walls. The doctor comes in in a trench coat and rubber gloves, barely nods to me. Despite now being legal, this all feels very back alley to me but without the wire hangers and surreptitious glances. The shame is only inside me.

The doctor tells me what to expect. He gives the nurse a flashlight, turns on the machine, and the noise is horrendous, wrathful. The light in the room turns eerie amber as the machine sucks all the power out of the generator. He numbs me, sedates me further with gentle words, inserts a cannula and, without ceremony, vacuums out the residue as I cramp, spasm, and emit the pulp of what little there was of it and its supply source, my blood, my lifeforce.

I thank the doctor, the nurse, and the new law for another chance at my own life until I'm woman enough, wise enough, loved enough by my own self, and ready enough to take on another.

HOLLYWOOD HIGH

It started on a January day in 1975 when I opened my disoriented eyes on the second floor of a run-down, four-story, rent-by-the-night flophouse called the Hollywood Hotel on Hollywood Boulevard.

I'd found it in the Yellow Pages at a pay phone at the Los Angeles airport when I first landed, and it had taken me nearly two hours to get there via a network of bus routes. Aging window shades sepia-toned the room, making everything in it, even me, seem like a tattering photo or fading film. Outside, traffic honked, and people hawked stuff on the street. It sounded like New York City. Comforting. I stretched and noticed I felt new, I felt different, I felt—what was it? I felt free. I could breathe. I was no longer living a lie. I felt fearless. Recognizing that my ex-boyfriend was a replicant of my crazy controlling daddy, I'd finally fled.

Dressing fast as a fireman, I pulled on panties, pants, socks, then shoes in two moves. I couldn't miss a minute. I grabbed my bag and key and hurtled down the dark hallway into the creaky elevator. I'd never been to Hollywood before, and I needed to find breakfast and see some sights before my big meeting with the big agent at 5:00 p.m. I burst though the shoddy lobby doors onto the teeming thoroughfare, into the bright January morning, hungry to understand where and who the hell I now might be.

The air was chilly, the winter sun hot. Grauman's Chinese was right across the street. Footprints of famous stars were beneath my unknown feet. In seconds beatific strangers were upon me like flies on feces, pamphleting me. I exuded that stranger in paradise naïveté, and they saw me as prey. They all seemed abnormally happy to me, and soon my fists were full of blessings from the Hare Krishnas, flyers from the Born Agains, warnings from Jehovah's Witnesses, some blessing me with love and Christ, others threatening me with God, Hell, eternal damnation. Then the bulletin of the Church of Scientology invited me to free breakfast right next door to the hotel. They won. I ducked into their meeting room, chairs filling with tourists and other lookie-loos on their way to the Hollywood Wax Museum, noshing on free croissants, slurping free coffee.

The content of their handouts on "The Way to Happiness" reminded me of the Success in Commercials seminar I had taken in NYC weeks before, about clearing away self-preoccupations and negative thoughts. They instructed attendees to "take care of yourself," and "be worthy of trust." But it also said, "honor and help your parents" and "seek to live with the truth." These precepts as applied to my family seemed completely contradictory. Living my truth would only dishonor them. Nonetheless, I pocketed the consciousness-friendly papers, planning to read them later, ducked out, diving deeper into crowds, so much like the mobs at Times Square drooling for sensation, only here swarms seemed to think they'd find or give spiritual awakening, too. Hollywood Boulevard was a paradoxical place, I mused.

I needed to get way above this fray. I turned and headed for the hills in the opposite direction. As the city energy decelerated, I took a right up onto a steep incline. Maybe I could lose a few pounds by 5:00 p.m. The abortion-abbreviated pregnancy a few months before had left me puffy, sluggish, and sad, my waistline missing out-of-action. So, I clambered up and up until verdant wild fields with northeastern trees invited me just past a slightly opened gate. I wandered in, amazed by the greenery and tumbledown estuary just a few blocks from the teeming metropolis. Gnats danced in sunbeams. Birdsong tickled my eardrums. California sure was gorgeous.

When I was a girl shoveling snow like Sisyphus for my pittance of an allowance, I'd hear my money-hungry father and his poker pals speak in a fervent hush of going west—not to pan for gold, but for big bucks in the silver screen businesses there. Dad was desperate to get to this promised land but groused that he had to take care of my sister, my mother, and me.

"Go west, young man, go west," my grandfather told my bachelor Uncle Jack, who had gone years ago. We got one postcard of the Hollywood sign from him, mentioning his deals, but no details on how to write him back. He'd fallen into some Hollywood pool that drowned out his need for my father.

"If you ever get out to California, find your Uncle Jack." Dad said. "When he wrote, he said he's in 'show business.' Maybe he can get you a little dancing job," he sneered.

Maybe he could help me escape my father's sarcasm.

I got to a higher vantage point, climbed atop a large rock on a hill, and stopped to gulp for breath. I turned to see where the hell I was and got gob-smacked.

A view of bluish snows draped atop a distant mountain range through a far-out pink mist to the east caressed my optic nerve. Between me and them were teeny spikes of city skyscrapers and twinkling suburbs, with highways snaking through, a muffled throb of car and plane engines merging into an orchestral roar. Inside my nostrils, the fragrances of wildflowers and grasses partied in defiance of winter. To the west lay a vast, unobstructed iron-gray-blue sea swimming out to infinity. Like towels tumbling gently in the dryer of a dream, this bombardment of images melted and merged into a thrilling new sensation, underscoring the vastest vista I had ever seen, the furthest horizon I had ever spied, caressing my brainstem into pleasure.

I was exhilarated beyond all my imaginings—beyond the claustrophobic Connecticut confines of the small rooms and minds I grew up with, beyond the view of the opposite shore there, bordered by the rocks and outcroppings of Long Island across the small pond of the sound, beyond the cityscapes of Manhattan, broader than the gray-toned Hudson River hemmed in by Hoboken, New Jersey, to the west, or the East River, abbreviated by Roosevelt Island to the east. It was like my forehead had gone 3-D Technicolor, Imax, my vision now unlimited. The dark weight I had always felt on my head on the East Coast, that ceiling pushing me down and down, was lifting on the West Coast. I was proud I'd made it all this way here on my own. Maybe the Atlantic had never been my sea. The Pacific was calling to me to linger by its side now.

And it hit me.

I felt happy.

I felt the miracle of breathing, exhaling only to instantly find and inhale air sufficient to sustain me. I felt wonderment that although I had nothing tangible—job, car, money, home, love, family, fitness, future—I felt rich, alive and free for the first time I could recall in my postnatal history. I sat in triumph to take it all in, to hoard it like nuts for imminent return of winter.

Wait. Couldn't I make this pleasure, this permission, last forever? Straining might scare it away.

I did not want to ever leave that rock, for fear I'd lose it all with the next step. I climbed slowly down, took two steps. Still there. Walked past the gate, down a block. Good! The feeling of ebullience endured as I headed all the way back past religious zealots and drooling tourists, to my cheap but atmospheric hotel room, as I prettied up for the many bus trips to my meeting.

I floated into that high-powered talent agency like I belonged. My optimism and confidence impressed the big-name agent enough that he arranged for an audition for me the very next day. I awoke one eye at a time in the same free-form mental state, bussed to CBS's studios, where I was welcomed through the gate, auditioned, did some improvisations, and got the job. Gravity-free, I did some sketches on a special with the Smothers Brothers the following day. One day's work, but a year's worth of my own credibility. If I did it once, damn it, I could do it again.

I was all aboard the joy boat for days. I had a T-shirt made down the street from my hotel that said, "Life Is Enough." I ate ambrosia in a health food store in wonderment. I browsed the materials at a spiritual bookstore and, like the Scientology handouts I read each night, grasped it all instantly. I was in a rarified state of instant enlightenment in which I understood it all. I sent postcards full of love to the few who would care to receive them. I called my mother.

"What. Are you high on drugs?" she asked.

"High on life, Mom," I said. "High on life."

How I wished I could turn my mother on, too, to save her from enslavement, but I couldn't slacken my voyage. I couldn't go back in to pull her out. I knew I'd either kill him or myself. It took me down a little to think of their chosen imprisonments in their Grand Guignol of a marriage. I would not handicap myself with some ball and chain of a husband around my neck like she had.

Just as my burgeoning feeling of peace and love began to swell my heart and enlarge my dreams, my fear it would fade arose. I feared that like a startled fawn it would withdraw into the forest with my scrutiny. I was leaving to return to my New York apartment the next day and wanted to hoard every second, like a person fleeing famine prolongs the rice. I stayed up all night to relish it.

And when my last morning came, it receded. I tried to grab on to its edges, identify where it was flickering in this room or this town. I vowed I'd come back to California to live in it. But I knew it wasn't in California. It had to be in me, and I was determined to take it to-go and have it everywhere. I pledged to mine this pinprick of bright light I'd seen so I could move and live in that bright new world.

HUSBANDRY

My younger sister had hurled her bridal bouquet right at me, and I'd caught it just as I had at her first wedding three years before. She was good both at marrying and pelting me with flowers. I envied her. At twenty-eight, I hardly knew myself well enough to know who'd best be mated with me. But now that I had twice caught the bouquet, every single single man I met might be possible.

I ached to be in forever love and tried to narrow down the choices and ignore the crushes I got so easily. Sometimes kissing a crush ruined the whole illusion. I'd learned that, for me, instant attraction was a poor harbinger, the most untrustworthy of drives. So, I imagined myself burrowing into hundreds of kinds of nice men's faces, diving past the chins, through the beards, deep into the zone between mouth and nose where carbon dioxide exhalation might have an irresistible scent, then I'd sample the lips. I would become a kiss connoisseur. I fantasized about stroking a million hairstyles, admiring a thousand chests and two thousand pairs of shoulders, seeing how far I could get past those into minds, hearts, and eyes. In my imagination, I tried them all on for size. This short one was so cute, but this big guy could carry me, protect me. This smart one could tell me how to live my life wisely, but the funny one would distract me from bad news. I liked funny—funny for me was like gorgeous for other women. The best one for me would have to be funny.

I'd find myself talking to my sister or close friends in my mind, as if reflecting back in time. I'd give a wistful sigh and say, "It was love at first sight."

Or

"We had an instant antipathy, but last week we realized we were meant for each other."

Or

"It took a while, but then we grew into each other, like vines nature tangles."

Or

"We were best friends for years, then he kissed me."

But those conversations couldn't occur in real life until I actually found the one.

It wouldn't be easy. I had lots to unlearn, and lots of money I needed to make so I would have my own power in a relationship. Having money and staying childfree as long as possible was the magical elixir that promised a woman wouldn't have to sell her soul or be beholden to some schmuck with a few bucks in a life of indentured masochism.

That's the mistake my mother had made. She had no choice. My dad looked like a big winner when she met him playing poker on Bagel Beach that Connecticut summer of '47. Handsome and popular, with beautiful brown eyes, he looked like Dane Clark, a television star at the time. Newly sprung from the service with a small stipend in the pocket of his swim trunks, he was ready to marry and asked her to lunch immediately.

Their wedding day picture from eight months later always gives me a damned good cry. I pull it out of the family album once in a while around their anniversary, as spring bitter-sweetens my brain. I mourn their marriage, which made me who I am yet thwarted who I might have been. I rue how beauty wastes away, how well-meaning hearts get broken, how hope disappears with the money. I imagine being there at the onset of their relationship.

It was a picture-perfect spring day, as it is now. He was good-looking, like in the movies good-looking, and boy, did he know it. Many girls, mostly gentiles, had batted their eyes and sashayed past him, laughing too loud when he came near, but this one had been the most interesting yet.

She was Jewish, but assimilated, with a nice American voice, no Yiddish accent like his parents had. Her dainty waistline and nervous giggle roused his feelings of manliness and patriotism. He could live with that giggle, he figured, as long as forever would last, which would probably be a lot longer now that the war was over.

He'd had a ball in the war in the Air Force, flying Boeings high in safe skies. Never got to the front as he hoped, because he got heartsick—rheumatic fever, they said, and he had a bad ticker after that. The Air Force gave him a nice cash allotment and a year of college, even threw in two free gravesites. He had a lot to offer a nice Jewish girl. He was flush.

He mashed his mouth hard into hers, for the wedding photographer, for their families, hoping sheer pressure, plus her pinup girl prettiness, could start some sparks between them. She kissed back but resisted wiggling her face back and forth the way she'd seen other girls kiss—after what had happened to her with the other man, she didn't want anyone to think she was easy, even now that she was married. Everybody oohed and ahhed with borrowed joy. She resisted the urge to wipe off his wetness, fearful of smearing her crimson lipstick or offending somebody. She just let his nice Jewish boy saliva dry her lips stiff.

She straightened her veil, stalling to see if she had any romantic feelings now that they were wed and she was safe. Nada. She didn't really know if the unease in her stomach was from love, but she clamped down her queasiness and smiled all day long, hard, for her family and his. Her poor parents, still running from the soldiers in the pogroms of their nightmares, still eating like pigs to make up for not having eaten for years. They deserved some happiness for putting up with all her problems. They also wanted grandchildren—immediately, as many as possible—and would bribe the bride and groom in the form of cash gifts from their meager budgets to make it happen maybe a little sooner than later, before, God forbid, somebody died.

She knew that a baby could never happen because she was broken inside, and she needed to make it up to them, and to her brand-new husband, for eloping with that other man three years before. That man had treated her rough on their wedding night.

"C'mon! It's okay," he'd told her when they got onto the double bed in their hotel room, and she covered up in shyness. "We're married."

But then he ripped into her rough, pushed on her hard, and covered her mouth when she cried out and froze underneath him in terror.

"What's the matter with you?" he hollered. "Stop acting like a dead doll—you're my wife now!"

He struck her, then, disgusted, he left her alone in a disinfected hotel room five miles but another world away from her parents' apartment, which smelled of chicken fat like the whole Old Country had. She had hoped the man would be her new harbor in New Haven and honor and protect her till death did them part.

But the way he parted her insides broke that idea pretty fast.

That guy left her lying in her first-time blood, and his mother came with a fur coat to the hotel, where the new bride had lain for days, mute, shaking, crazed.

His mother told the girl, "I'll give you this fur coat if you give my son a divorce right away."

Her silence mistaken for agreement, the fur coat was left, then taken as payment by the desk clerk for her hotel stay.

She had thought she would be annulled forever from married life, as she was ruined and had been given electroshock treatments until she pretended to get well to make it stop and was sent home to her angry parents—the worst place for a damaged, fragile young woman. She had thought her life was over until she met this new man at Bagel Beach. He took her for kosher hot dogs and French fries down the coast. Her friends thought he was very attractive and seemed polite. He asked her to marry him on their fifth date after a movie with Tyrone Power, who looked like him, the girls said. She was so shocked and grateful, she wept as she said maybe, feeling she should first tell him everything. One night over Chinese food, she did.

"Nobody knows this but you. I think he broke me," she said. "I don't think I can ever have kids."

He darkened. He wasn't sure exactly what she meant, but he thought it over for a few minutes while she went into the powder room and looked in the mirror to see if she was still there. She fixed her face, fearing the end. She came out scared, but he was beaming.

"Hey, it's okay," he said. "I'll be the kid in the family!"

So, with the shul already booked and everyone invited, she had intercourse with him a week before the wedding, to make sure she could do it, to prove she'd do anything to be worth a new life. He was gentle and kind. He didn't push. And she felt obligated to be a good wife, if she couldn't be a mother. He didn't know yet that she couldn't cook.

But little did they know. I'm in the picture already, the surprise to come. Behind the three-tiered cake with the little bride and groom on top, under her wedding suit skirt, while they're posing kissing for the camera, I'm dividing fast as I can into many cells, deep in the bride's belly. I'll make my big entrance eight months and two weeks after their wedding day, so no one will ever really know I'm a lucky bastard. I'll be my parents' pride and joy for a time, then their burden.

This photograph is the only proof I have that my parents ever even kissed. After I'm born a girl and not the boy he really wanted, they'll only touch each other that way again maybe a few times in their fertile bed of determination to make this life and their love work to make another baby. After they got that, my mother would make it stop, cutting off her beautiful hair, covering up her body, never wearing lipstick again.

So, at twenty-eight, I shut down my dreaming of weddings and getting swept off my feet for a long while. I longed for company but would have to fight my ravenous hunger to attach, to enmesh with or without love. I shut down any possibility of pregnancy with a battery of paraphernalia and pills now available so we women could be safer to work in the world while exploring and fending off men, so we could feel protected if we ever went all the way—until I could make decisions from a solid center. I hoped it wouldn't be long till the time was right, because my drive to get romantic was irrepressible.

MY OBSCURED THIRD EYE

I was twenty-nine, pretty, earning a living, getting famous, and I was losing my mind. Compulsive thoughts were straining the fissures of my skull, and I had no idea how to get helped. Somewhere over the rainbow, Judy Garland had once been a coddled goddess for her public nervous breakdowns. But these days the nervously broken-downs were scorned and stigmatized, fodder for the tabloids in the entertainment world.

Maybe I could quietly check into a hospital to contain myself. There doctors would prescribe, medications would dull, and insurance would cover a breakdown. But I was scared to get swept up in a medical system that had made a mess of my father's heart. And I couldn't risk my regular role on one of the big three networks, the series a hit at the end of its first season and picked up for another. This was my first-ever TV contract with an ongoing if modest salary. I couldn't jeopardize the recognition, the opportunities, and especially the work—life's blood for a ravenous actor. Scooping out my brain and splatting it on the sidewalk now would be ill-timed, especially after how hard I'd worked to become an overnight success.

I'd spent a few years in the trenches of stand-up on the East Coast, moonlighting after theater performances of a Sondheim musical off-Broadway, an operetta at the Village Gate, a Molière play on Broadway. As I was one of the few women both standing up and singing my offbeat novelty songs, club owner Budd Friedman would have me open before Andy Kaufman or close after David Brenner, both deathtrap spots for comedians. He'd put me on after Robin Williams on the West Coast, and I'd be slipping in Robin's sweat, trying to make the most of the leftover laughs from his loosened-up audiences. Now I was grateful to be making baby steps toward a livelihood. I could no longer make ends meet doing theater alone.

After rounds of auditions for ABC's answer to *Saturday Night Live*, called *Fridays*, there were final screen tests involving improvs with soloist scene-eaters who controlled rather than collaborated. I didn't get the job—the wife of one of the ABC execs was hired. Then, after weeks of smoking dope, pigging out, and settling in for a long, maudlin depression, I got two hours' notice to report to ABC Studios to replace the wife. I jumped in, late and logy, after the talented cast had already gelled into an ensemble, after characters had already been developed.

Despite feeling off-balance, I always showed up punctually and prepared for the six-day-a-week schedule. I spent the seventh day developing new material that was mostly nixed by the male staff, as were all the ideas generated by the women cast members, while Larry David and Michael Richards's male-centric material was welcomed. While I appeared funny and friendly on set, keeping up my façade meant crying in restroom stalls, bellowing in my car, thrashing in my bed, fragmenting in the middle of me.

If my madness were made public, people would assume it was caused by the onset of celebrity, making me feel isolated amid hordes of fans. True, the impersonal adulation and salacious fan mail from prison inmates was weird. My friends' and family's reactions to my incipient fame were even weirder. My own intimidated mother glazed over and giggled about nothing in my presence. Other family members mistook my exhaustion for disinterest in them and retaliated by ignoring me back.

Old friends wore me like a status symbol on the one hand and prickled with envy on the other, lashing out in unpredictable ways. There's nothing like a loved one's success to make one's own life feel like shit. My arrival seemed to be provoking breakdowns in intimates I desperately needed to stay stable. I developed nice-lady Tourette's, rapid-firing compliments to disarm people—"gorgeous hair," "great eyes," "so handsome"—before their discomfort could set in, to get the focus off myself. My visibility was such a contrast to the invisible outcast identity I'd felt since girlhood, which I had begun performing to counter. Now I felt like a bigger oddity, but still not at one with people.

But this predictable stress was surpassed in spades by the sexy, witty writer who'd first followed me home from our pilot pickup celebration. As our show ratings rose and he slipped over that fine line from comic genius to coke-addled maniac, I tried to anchor myself in my role as his savior. He'd collapse and reconstitute from his highs in my arms, which I mistook for adoration. Nights felt so good, but the hangover in my heart hurt bad at work, where he'd pretend we weren't involved.

Once he was made head writer, we couldn't get away from each other, working crazy close too many hours a day, too many days a week. He'd watch me on the overhead TV monitors rehearsing scenes he'd written. I'd get his picayune notes on how best to deliver his lines, as he rewrote my own writing. Resentment and attachment throbbed in tandem in our bodies. The only way to escape each other was to have sex with each other—every single night.

We spent all season murmuring yes in the dark, muttering no in the light. My hunger to attach to something solid as the sands shifted beneath my feet got me more and more mired in this horny human sinkhole. I learned too late that his ex-girlfriend had a nervous breakdown and attempted suicide when she heard we were an item. Oh, this guy was a card-carrying crazy-maker.

Facing a two-month spring break from him and the series, I fled to what had always been my most healing place—my New York acting class. My first night back, I began to blubber reading a scene from a Neil Simon play—a dead giveaway. After class I was approached by a sympathetic classmate.

"I feel your pain," she murmured. "Let's talk outside."

I instantly made this kind stranger, let's call her Laurel, my confidante. I told her I felt split, false, scared, with nowhere to hide in my newly minted recognizability.

"Oh my God," Laurel said. "You're, like, having a spiritual crisis."

Spiritual crises were what the severely rich and famous and the press called their breakdowns. The resulting spiritual trans-formations had an artistic, sincere patina, and led to dropping out, dropping acid, and other adventures scored by sitar music, scented by incense. Spiritual journeys were costly and required drastic wardrobe and location changes and long-term commit-ments to one monotonal way of being while moaning "Ohm." I didn't want to let go of the varieties of selves I carried inside me. And my TV work didn't afford me the time or money for travel to India, to get tutelage and the trappings of spirituality. I couldn't drop out of my new life—I had just dropped in.

But I had experienced so few moments of unearned joy in my life that I was questioning the purpose of my existence and why acting was my everything. Marrying and motherhood and traveling the real world were on a very back burner as I profited from the imagined worlds. Seeking inner peace was a hobby I always sidelined until unbearable pain set in. I had achieved peace in meditation for maybe a minute in the ten or so classes I'd taken. It had happened accidentally for a few days once with no effort. I had dabbled in many talks and books about seeing reality differently, which I could easily do as an actor, if not as myself, whatever the hell that was.

"I don't know . . . ," I said.

"What does your inner voice say?" asked Laurel.

I told her my inner voice had laryngitis lately, sounding more like a soulful Barry White than anything vaguely spiritual.

"You must meet Baba Muktananda," she said. "He saved my life."

I'd read of this renowned guru and his power to heal minds. As she spoke of her hallowed teacher, it seemed serendipitous that his meetup center was one block from my New York apartment and that his upcoming five-week retreat in the country, starting in ten days, coincided mystically with the months I'd be on hiatus from the show. I was in deep need of a perspective change, to see through my blinded third eye, to winnow down all my voices to a single coherent one. Plus natural air and light in my face after months of incarceration in a windowless, fluorescent-lit, air-conditioned funny farm of funny men could be nothing but healthy.

"Oh, come on, baby—let's go," Barry White whispered.

It was meant to be. Synchronicity, serenity, Siddhartha, sandalwood, Satsang, plus Siddha Yoga—all the *s* sounds associated with spiritual retreat sounded heaven-sent. All fell quickly, mystically into place. Laurel arranged for me to be bussed from the

New York City meetup center to the Shree Muktananda Ashram, formerly the Brickman Hotel and Nightclub in the Catskills. As that was where my comedy career had begun, it seemed fitting that my drive to be funny might end there, too. A springtime ride into the mountains alone could heal me.

The next morning, I stepped aboard a bus with twenty normal-seeming fellow passengers, who began a monotonous Hare Krishna chant as soon as we crossed the Hudson. I'd always felt unnerved by people all speaking the same words in the same voice at the same time. I never fit into the choruses of Broadway shows; song and dance simultaneity was not in my repertoire. Similarly, a one-size-fits-all faith felt implausible to me. I was raised as a devout atheist. I'd not yet been able to park my mind with any one deity or guru or philosophy, although I'd been sampling their books and tapes mix 'n match for years while studying yoga.

As we pulled into the ashram's circular driveway and the zoned-out passengers disembarked, I felt far nuttier, my disorientation worsened. The Brickman's venerable prewar building had been painted a Day-Glo, space-age hue of blue. And where once loomed headshots of Shecky Greene, Mort Sahl, and other Borscht Belt headliners on poles by the pool, now towered hallowed portraits of the late great gurus of the time—Paramahansa Yogananda, and Muktananda's own teacher, Bhagavan Nityananda.

I saw Laurel in the lobby barefoot in a toga. Though her eyes were in a state of beatific bliss, her emaciated body looked like hell. The red pigment swabbed on her third-eye point matched her rash-covered skin. As I approached, she bowed.

"Hello, Laurel," I said, and cautiously. "How are you?"

"Call me Kalika," she said. "Baba has renamed me for the Hindu goddess. He's put me on a fast of bread and milk to overcome my allergies to them."

"Uh-*huh!*" was the most neutral thing I could think of to say.

"I got you an audience with Baba first thing in the morning," she said, "so you gotta get an offering at the guest store."

Kalika/Laurel brought panicky me and my pricey rattan yellow-ribboned fruit basket upstairs to a suite with a view of the mountains and a thronelike toilet in a large bathroom that echoed my offerings too audibly. Hollywood hype had spread to this sanctified space, too. I feared my sudden press-worthiness would be exploited and something unsavory demanded in return.

"STOP IT," I yelled at my doubt. "Receive the gift!"

"Oh, so beautiful, baby," said Barry.

Kalika/Laurel rushed me down to the Big Room off the main lobby, where Vegas headliners had once spewed one-liners. Someone rang a bell, and folks fell to their knees and began the Hare Krishna chant, trancing out. Some sat still in full lotus position, some swayed. I sat for a stretch, pretending to chant. Soon, with a perfectly lovely carpet in front of me, I did enough mindless mumbling to justify stretching face first onto the carpet in a yogic Child's Pose. Then I napped in its immaculate nap, lulled by the closeness of others. How nice to be able to sleep with other people without having sex first.

Then I heard a hush of excitement rippling through the room. "Baba's coming," people whispered. "It's Baba."

"Don't look at him—just, like, feel him," Kalika/Laurel said.

But I snuck a peek as the little old man in orange robes wafted from the rear of the Big Room to the front, mumbling incantations over the crowd. He tapped a few people on the head with a peacock feather wand, which cast them into paroxysms of joy. He sat on the dais on the main stage, gazing at us as the chant droned on, and I fell back into a sweet stupor.

Later, as the sun set behind the ashram's lush mountain views, the Krishna chant rose again from hundreds of voices in the Big Room below my room and continued long into the night. I fell into a fitful sleep, integrating the drone into the tapestry of a too-vivid dream: I saw chanting acolytes sitting in passive repose as a detached Baba took liberties with me on a gynecological table. Red light was emanating from his gaping third eye. I awoke with a silent scream of shame. How horrible—not just the dream, but this twisted sister brain that created it. Boy, did I need a psychic colonic. I truly hoped Muktananda would ignore my mistrust and fix me.

After a silent breakfast of grains and nuts, my crunching deafening in the absence of chitchat, Kalika/Laurel and her nasty full-body rash ushered me through a golden door off the lobby labeled *Media Room*. There sat about thirty people, among them a well-known TV news anchor and crew, and the singer John Denver. So much for escaping into an alternate universe. Hope's silly glimmers were draining fast from me. My negatives tidal-waved in. I realized I might need to escape from this escape.

We sat down on the plush rug. Nut-brown Baba, seated on a satin tuffet with a beautiful, sari-clad Indian woman translating to his right, was blessing an older man, who bowed to the ground and slid blissfully backward, cheeks wet with tears, into the circle of observers. Then, Kalika/Laurel nudged me and shoved my fruit basket forward, and I humbly crawled alongside it to face the guru and his glamorous translator. I felt like an imposter in this place of privilege.

"Why have you come?" the woman asked in a deep and sensuous voice. Baba eyed me mischievously as he fanned himself with the peacock wand.

I swallowed my urge to drown them in weepy words and summarized my turmoil.

"Please tell him my mind is broken. I am very unhappy."

The lovely woman translated, and he babbled back to her in an Indian dialect.

"Baba says you must stay and meditate with us here at the ashram for the year," she said.

"Um, tell him thanks, but I have to be back at work in July." I was so hoping the speed-read version of enlightenment could be instilled by July 8. I'd pay extra, I explained.

There was a quick back and forth before she said, "Baba says your peace is here."

"But I'm on contract, see, and there wouldn't be any peace for many people or me if I broke it," I stammered.

Were they going to take me captive? My agents would be furious.

"The work of ending your suffering must be here with Baba," she said.

"But see, if I left the TV show, me and others would suffer big consequences. Hey, maybe he could come out to the studio in California and heal us all!" My smartass persona was working too hard to save face in front of the press.

Baba seemed to be meditating on the possibility of that, or maybe just contemplating the sincerity of my seeking. Grandly, he gestured to Kalika/Laurel behind me.

"Can you give her a job on your show?" the interpreter asked on his behalf, on her behalf.

"Well," I said, "I'm not really in a position to hire Kalika. I could recommend her, but see, uh, she'd have to come back to Los

Angeles and put on some weight . . ."

Suddenly, he smote me on the head with the peacock wand. The group gasped. I froze but had the presence of mind to open to the possibility of externally applied enlightenment, his awakening of my Kundalini energy, his opening of my third eye, his goldening of my aura. I inhaled the incense, breathed it real deep. Oh, at heart, I wanted it so bad. I was starving for a mind change, to perceive things and myself differently, to dissolve my ego. *Please, please, please,* I prayed, but to what? Barry White? I begged my own agony to let me go.

The whole room held its collective breath—those few seconds passed like years. I hungrily surveyed my body and brain for transformation. Was I blessed by an instant fix? Moved to change my life, my outlook, to give up acting, comedy, clothes, vanity, meat, sex, money?

I felt nothing—just like that dancer girl sang in *A Chorus Line.*

Then Barry White stage-whispered in my ear, "You gotta go now, baby. Go now."

I bowed, then crawled/scampered backward. Others scanned my face for transcendence, finding it inscrutable. Then somebody else's pricey fruit basket from the gift shop was shoved forward, and Baba's playful gaze was on to the next and I was persona non grata.

As I rushed down from retrieving my things from the VIP suite, I saw my rattan gift basket with the yellow ribbon being returned to the ashram shop, apparently for resale to eager acolytes awaiting their turn for an audience. I was aware of the ache of disappointment flooding my body.

And as hordes of new devotees poured off the shuttle bus, I

boarded it alone for the trip back to New York City. Although I was relieved to be leaving, a heaviness rekindled in my belly. I was sad that I was resistant to the gifts of the mountains, Baba, and Laurel. That this misery was guru-proof. I would have to heal my mind some other way.

Tape by tape, teacher by teacher, *A Course in Miracles* lesson by lesson, I'd hold it together through many stages of madness while working full-time in Hollywood in the public eye. As more and more strangers feasted on the facsimile of my face filtered through a TV screen, I struggled to belong more to myself than to them.

Months later, Baba Muktananda died, and I read that scandal had erupted at the ashram. Apparently, Baba, while fostering abstinence and celibacy, had repeatedly forced sex as a "blessing" upon young female disciples—including Kalika/Laurel—on just such a table as I had nightmared that night. Baba's community was soon in chaos, his legacy tainted. His beautiful translator wrested control from her brother in a violent conflict, becoming the new Gurumayi.

I had an ah-ha moment. While Muktananda's legacy of healing was retroactively vulgarized, my gut instinct to flee was validated. So I did get a gift from the journey. And as my self-recrimination quieted, my inner voice grew stronger and more trustworthy, sounding a lot less like Barry White, the spokesperson for my escapism, and a lot more like a mature me, the spokesperson for my sanity.

Knowing I had trustworthy intuitions if I would only listen, the hatch to mental health was pried open, and my spiritual healing began . . . again.

HOMING IN

After three high-pressure years on a sound stage, on camera, in artificial bright light, in cold conditioned air, I felt denatured.

I was exhausted by my dreams which all took place on stages and sets with puppeteers behind the scenes, and I was both the puppets and the puppeteers. If called upon to enact human emotions in new roles I probably wouldn't remember them sufficiently to resource them. I'd been satirizing human feelings in sketch work for years.

My instincts had gotten further scrambled by studio audiences who flapped and barked like performing seals to get themselves on camera, rather than genuinely responding. I had no sense of how I came across unless I got honest-to-goodness belly laughs. My false front was facing inside me, too.

I had career choices for the first time, and my agents were impatient to know what the hell was next for me. I pulled back from their pressure and listened hard for soul signals. My inner voice, while no longer sounding like soul singer Barry White, was faint and almost monosyllabic, intelligible only as a quiet "no" to a horror movie role, "not now" to a sitcom role. It stayed mum about life choices, like it was beneath its purview.

But then I was offered the female lead in the West Coast

premiere of an off-Broadway hit musical called *March of the Falsettos* at a big Los Angeles theater. The story contained in the score and lyrics was quirky yet clear without fancy-schmancy special effects. I adored the four other male cast members, who'd done the show in New York. I knew this sort of thing would not come along often, and my inner voice, as I interpreted it, insisted, "YES." I knew being back in the bosom of a real-live theater audience in sustained scenes could be a healing first step.

The three weeks of rehearsal away from cameras was rehabilitating, and I was happy to be breaking in the composer-lyricist's tour de force new song, "I'm Breaking Down." As I was having a full-on breakdown myself at the time, it was the perfect place to park my turmoil, to channel my crazies, to make them tolerable by sending them up for comic effect. This catharsis through art was "cathartistic."

Opening-night telegrams and flowers were arriving for us when a large package festooned with multicolored ribbons was delivered to the stage door by a messenger, addressed to me. Strange sounds were emitting from it, so the guys and I tore off the wrapping paper to reveal a large birdcage containing a live carrier pigeon, a wheel of gouda, a bottle of Dom Pérignon, and a bag of birdseed. I was baffled, but the overture was starting, so we ran to the stage.

As our opening night show wrapped to a standing ovation, the others and I rushed upstairs, flushed with our success, to open the pricey champagne for a toast and to read the note attached to the cage.

"I'm a big fan, and a humble farmer. I own and operate my own ranch and brewery in North Texas. Here are photos of me on my property."

Several snapshots hung in the cage, revealing a ruddy, be-spectacled gentleman of about fifty dwarfed by farm animals in front of large stables and brewery buildings in the midst of a vast acreage—plus his business card.

"I'll be bold and tell you I'm looking for a wife to share my world. I have more than enough to care for someone and could support your career, too. I would enjoy coming along on your life.

"I'm attending your Saturday matinee in eight weeks and would like the opportunity to take you to supper afterward at the Brown Derby. If you agree to meet me, write a note with your "Yes" and attach it to the leg of my prize homing pigeon, inside the enclosed ring. If you are romantically involved and prefer not to meet, write "No" on the note and set her free to fly back to me. She has made the flight from Los Angeles in the past and knows her way home."

I wondered how many return trips this pigeon had made from LA carrying nos back from other actresses.

"Either way, I know I'll enjoy seeing you onstage. Have a good show. It was signed, Respectfully, Dudley."

This was the most original, attention-getting fan mail I'd ever gotten. It beat out the red nightgown sent by the crew of the nuclear sub the USS *Bremerton* that had been emblazoned with *Submariners Do It Deeper* on the front, and all the novel proposi-tions by prisoners. But I was in no spirit for any full-court press, especially from some stranger bribing me with livestock. I knew I'd be too fragmented, too mixed up about who I was and what I wanted to entertain proposals of any ilk for a very long time.

My four male costars found it all hilarious and, lonely for their lives and wives back in New York, insisted I say yes to lunch at the Derby so they could come along and watch our scene play out from behind some ferns. I already knew it would be no to Dudley, but delayed demurring because I was getting a loud yes from inside myself to the pigeon I named Midge.

Midge became our show's good luck charm and my personal sedative—an organic element among the trappings of theatricality, which, although less denatured than television studios, were still one step removed from life. Over the next weeks, she flapped less, cooed more, and so did I, as she pecked away at her seed in her cage, first in my dressing room, and on our days off in her vacation quarters at my apartment. I loved having her company.

After a long five-week delay, I broke it to the guys that I'd have to say no by bird to meeting Dudley. They whined, felt deprived, called me heartless. I asked them to join me at my third-floor dressing room window before the matinee the next day for the ceremonial setting free of Midge, so she could fly my dismissive missive home. I had held a trusting someone's personal property hostage and had to let go. I recognized what setting this pet free would cost me.

I wrote no on the little note, and as the guys held Midge gently by her soft sides, I affixed it into the ring on her leg. I kissed her bouncy little head fondly, leaned out the window, and tossed her hard up into the sky over the Huntington Hartford Theatre parking lot. We four hung out the window to watch her arc into the sky.

I got gooseflesh. She was so much bigger with her wings spread. Valiant, she flapped hard, getting some ballast on the wind, but then couldn't seem to soar aloft. We began to panic, frantic, cheering her on as folks getting out of cars below to attend the show looked up at all the commotion.

After struggling in midair for what seemed an eternity,

Midge simply stopped trying. And then she dropped, gathered speed, and, plummeting like a stone, pelted a Cadillac hood right in front of an older couple. They screamed. A broken heap of her plumage on their car and our collective horror was all that remained of our Midge.

I wept apologies into the wind, to her, to the couple, to the cast, to Dudley, stricken sick at heart. I, an animal lover of the first order, longing for far more real life, had murdered Midge.

The show had to go on that day, with our spirits also failing to lift aloft. My out-of-control rendering of the "I'm Breaking Down" number stopped the show, and as people cheered, my soul sickness kept me from feeling their positive response. Afterward, I sent the parking attendant money to wash the couple's Caddy of pigeon remains, and to bring me two tail feathers. There was no time for ceremony or sentimentality, but the guys kept me company as I called Dudley's number on the pay phone to break the news.

He was happy to hear from me, until I told him of Midge's unfortunate death. He was silent on the line for a time.

"She was my prized pigeon's second squab, and her actual name was Number Three. She was used to regular exercise. No surprise she didn't make it after five weeks sitting locked up in the cage," he reproached.

"I'm horribly sorry," I said. "She was a wonderful, wonderful bird, and everybody here simply loved her."

"Irreplaceable," he said.

"I'm sure," I said.

"So? What was your answer?" Dudley asked. "Will you be having supper with me?"

"It was yes," I lied, "but listen, why don't I treat you to supper on that matinee day? It's the least I can do."

"Okay," he said, appeased.

When the day arrived, ruddy-faced Dudley came to the stage door in a three-piece suit. It wouldn't have mattered if he'd been diabolically handsome, which I knew he wouldn't be, as desirable men rarely work that hard at courtship. I introduced him around for condolences from the cast and crew and solemnly presented him with one of Midge's feathers. We told him what a comfort she had been and how fortunate he was to be her owner.

He thanked us but said that to him she was a working animal, utilitarian machinery serving his business (and his love life, I figured). Although relieved he didn't feel her loss as keenly as I did, I liked him even less.

We wordlessly chewed a couple of loud Cobb salads at the Brown Derby—it was beyond awkward. Despite being complimented on my performance by others at the restaurant that day, I was glutted with every possible nuance of despondency a person could have. Dudley was not the man to whom I could express it.

Having so fatally scrambled my Midge's homing instincts, I wondered if I'd ever come home to myself.

LADY GRIEF

Just as the Maui mists became an insistent drizzle, the bitch caught up with me in my VIP suite.

Lady Grief had stalked me for days, trying to slow me down with trailers of all my sob stories—why couldn't he, why didn't I—followed by a double feature of despair. She reminded me of every loss, every injustice, every hurt I ever had, straining my insides to seep out through my seams. I hoped my perfect eye makeup could hold her at bay.

It was easy to drown her out during daylight on this press junket, with many opportunities to be fully "on": posing at a charity event, eating out with executives, over-animating, smiling so hard my face and belly ached with contradiction. In the daytime, I could put on lip gloss to distract, sunglasses to cover up. At dusk I could slip out of her clutches, proud at how fast I could dodge and how many distractions I could create to fend her off, fearing I'd collapse if she caught me.

Wouldn't it be better to stop pushing so hard when you feel so very soft inside?

Fighting her and the furies off gave me a dynamic personality as I engaged with hotel guests over exotic fruited drinks at Happy Hour. But as pink evening morphed to soggy night, and guests politely slipped away into their own posh slots, ebullience was not so easy; this not so happy an hour.

I reflected on why the hell I was so good at deception. I could be so witty when I was suffering, my words a desperate counter-measure against terror, my persona constructed to distract me from unspeakable despair. I learned that craft, the discipline of creating these new selves, with help from experts.

Studying drama with Stella Adler in New York, I learned to immerse myself in an imaginary story, my self-consciousness va-porizing, finding it the greatest drug trip of an escape, taking the audience along on my human experience of written circumstanc-es. In drama, I didn't pretend, I *was*. Drama was my panacea, comedy a coping strategy. Doing comical sketches and plays, I was always 60 percent aware of the audience, 40 percent working it for effect. Diving deep in plays, I was 90 percent oblivious to anyone or anything outside the experience, except for the 10 per-cent of me that had to hit my marks, which knew when the lights dimmed and it was time to exit, or when lights blazed up to bow. I loved it.

Boy, I hadn't thought this deeply maybe ever. Isolated, unoc-cupied time, especially on weekends, was anathema to me. I'd al-ways dreaded Saturday nights shut in alone in my room. It seemed like all other humans had approving playmates with whom they could enjoy a night out each week, sleeping in on Sunday morn-ing until noon. I rarely did. I always sought a boyfriend to make Saturday into Sunday seamless. Between boyfriends, my in-ner assassins were too available to keep me company. Since last week's sudden end to a three-year roller-coaster romance, I was regressing, and Lady Grief was waiting to babysit.

Nothing better to see or do but to be with me tonight.

But, but, but—I'd planned to consume Hawaii's over-the-top

wonders this last Saturday evening on the island. I'd stroll by the sea, have a Shiatsu massage, and take native dance lessons. Maybe hula women with gorgeous gyrating hips could teach me how to hold a grass skirt up on my skimpy frame. I'd do anything to avoid the empty pointlessness of time spent alone with myself in a luxury hotel, in a VIP suite in paradise. What a waste having all this privilege for me alone.

I could write wish-you-were-here postcards, but there was no one I wished were here. I could take pictures off the balcony to show someone who might be interested, but they'd think I was gloating in my lap of luxury, alias hellhole. Wait. Maybe I could harness this turmoil artistically. There must be roles I could play for which I needed to know this pain. Or I could write a story. Nah. Who the hell would want to read a downer like this? I felt like Winnie in Beckett's play *Happy Days*, so desperate to fill vacant time, I'd construct causes. I'd clean the detritus from my purse, floss flotsam from my teeth, buff my nails, try to forget that life was an empty vacuum we strain to shape. We had no control. We would survive, then die alone and disintegrate into recyclable atoms like every human ever had.

Stop being so mean to yourself and to me.

Assessing myself in the bathroom mirrors, I looked pretty, but hard. Tense muscles around my eyelids were inadequate for display. I'd borrow an umbrella, go for a walk. I'd crank up my gift of gab and trip into a local dive, make conversation with folks who actually lived here, who actually liked eating poi and pineapple every damn day. Did anyone who lived here walk by the sea, or did they just take it all for granted? Were they all poseurs pretending to love this lush Eden they had gotten so over years ago? Were they bored to tears pretending to be grateful for us tourists? I made a rush for the door.

Where would you go?

And Lady G. overtook me, seducing me down, down, down, with my room key clutched in my hand. I panicked, panted, struggled. The illusion of salvation seemed to be just outside this room, this hall, this building, this body, this brain. She murmured, *I've got Nature's arms around you now.*

Breezes bearing her fragrance overtook misery in the middle of me. Rain drummed on the roof—ironic timing. A glut of hopelessness rushed up my gut like hot lava. Then came shame, fear for having tears, for losing control, for smearing my lip line. I began to weep from deeper down, drowning in my own deluge.

As I convulsed in sounds I hadn't heard from myself before, she brought me gently to my knees. Still self-conscious in front of my judgmental self, I pondered who or what the hell I was as I wept, hearing myself evolve from single-celled whimpers to fetal bleats, then infantile cries, then bellows of rage. Then the sounds matured, and I joined the timeless keening of millions of women who have lost their men, to war, to illness, by betrayal of them by him, or him by them, or by them betrayed by their own selves—like me. Layers of prehistoric hurts lined up to take a turn, circled to land like planes at a major hub as Lady Grief brought 'em in like air traffic control.

After a very long time, the furies faded. My mind was clearing. I stilled. I sniffed around. Lady Grief must be napping nearby because I felt nurtured, safe. I purred in the plush pillows. Nice to have no schedule. No one expecting me. Nowhere to be till the airport at 2:00 p.m. on Sunday.

Forgiveness no longer conceptual, I could forgive the ones I accused of trying to break me. I could pat myself on the mind, forgive myself for foisting the same suicide-by-bad-boyfriend phenomenon on myself again. Maybe this would be the night that began my real life, that made this peace inside more important than the instability my need for male-injected love caused. Then Maui sent a bathwater breeze in through the balcony doors. The king-sized bed, minus any king, in the master suite, minus any master, was meant for me alone. I deserved it. Time to fill it. I took off all my clothes. I spread out in the vast bed under its incredibly soft cover, conquering its incredible coolness, pushing my legs out to its enormous entirety. I focused on the unadulterated sensuous pleasure of incredibly tender sheets caressing me, asking nothing back. There would be no performance tonight.

Having emptied the bamboo box of free tissues, wearing an emblem of unblotted tears of grace on my face, I anointed myself with all the emollients in the toiletries basket in my boudoir and inhaled myself. I smelled damned good. I had good chemistry with me.

I stepped out on the balcony naked in the warm mist, hearing murmurs wafting from the suite next door as two people nestled inside. It didn't hurt to hear them. It didn't shut me out. I opened my arms to embrace them, was cleansed by a merciful breeze the same temperature as my body, and I could feel Paradise. I apologized to myself for being away so long—most of my life, in fact, except for a few accidental moments here and there when I loved myself for no damn reason.

As a vain, full moonlit night adorned herself with multicolored strands of clouds, I knew that this earth, this life, was meant for lovers, but it was also meant for me.

THE GREAT UNKNOWN

It was never fame or beauty or glamour or money that awed me, that attracted me. It was talent, on the page, on the stage, on the screen, in the ear, eye, and mind. The kind of talent that held me still, then propelled me to my feet to applaud; moved me to tears, to grow; made my belly laugh; and made my mind think, was that bigger-than-life, beyond the norm, viscera-shifting sort of power. You know it when you feel it.

Maybe this power was a compilation of nature-given gifts, or a spiritual calling. Or maybe the force of such talent was a desperate overcompensation born of striving and straining to get unavailable early love, using whatever the hell worked. Maybe both.

For me it was both, but I truly believed I had the talent part. I could feel it bubbling up sometimes when I could get my father out of my face—a confluence of imagination and liquidity and burning desire tempered by certainty. I knew it was raw and needed training, practice, discipline, fitness, energy, and protection. I knew that bigger-than-me extra something that came from a secret spot deep inside needed support. I knew it could move people to smiling through tears, making me feel like the expression of my feelings mattered to people in the right rooms. It made me feel love inside, for people, for myself. It made me feel part of the normal world.

I got in line at the Seventy-Second Street at Broadway news kiosk. I jostled someone, who stiffened in self-protection. I said sorry, then looked up to see it was John Lennon with his Yoko. They lived down the block at the Dakota. In caps and scarves, they were enjoying being like regular people out for an evening stroll. My face paralyzed, and a tingling shot up my underarms. I tried to appear unaffected, but they noticed me noticing and tensed, too—it's how they must have always felt mingling with us masses. I put down coins, struggled to say something pithily worthy of his gift, spun, and left without the paper, heart pounding, face pulsing all the way home. If someone had told me I'd be speaking aloud John's lyrics to "Imagine" live on national television the night of John's murder right down the block eight years later, I'd have said, "Don't talk crazy."

By day, I was a plainclothes temp typist with occasional auditions during lunch. At night I was a plainclothes performer thriving with an improv troupe. It was a low-risk, no-pay job at a poor man's theater, basically lights-up, lights-down on an empty space. We conjured locations, props, costumes, and characters by imagination only, without special effects. Improvisation felt to me like the finest pure art, combining all the other performing arts. You could shove almost any gifts into it, it was such a huge canvas. Writing, acting, dancing, and singing improvs with good players made my self-consciousness vaporize.

We were booked at a club called Gerde's Folk City, and the infamous comic/club owner Rodney Dangerfield loomed large right up front in a gray suit, in a room full of hippie folk singers and scruffy comics. I watched Rodney from the back sipping a scotch as he watched Jewish, waifish Richard Lewis. Lewis was deploring his father's artful fart ventriloquism, making his flatulence project like it was coming from his mother. I saw Rodney nod often, then jerk upright to applaud with the crowd, saying, "Oh yeah—terrific."

As Richard came anxiously offstage, I mouthed, "Dangerfield dug you!" He wrinkled up his cute nose to suppress his delight with his customary cynicism in his funny, complicated way.

Then it was our turn. Taking audience suggestions, we endowed each other with story, exaggerated our voices and body language to make scenes fly funny. I was set up a lot, unlike at girls' basketball practice where I never got the ball and was often trampled. Out of the corner of my eye, I couldn't help but see Rodney nod and snap up to clap whenever the crowd did, muttering, "Terrific. Oh, yeah. Great."

Egged on, I extended my bits, flying into spontaneous, inspired new territory, getting a big response from the crowd. And as we gathered for a bow, I looked to Rodney only to see that he was nodding off to sleep—as he continued to do all evening for every single act and had probably done for Richard—then jerking up to join the applause.

"Oh, yeah. Terrific." Silly me. Just thinking he approved made me fly. I was so easy.

Acting served so many purposes for me. I had a drive to take as many people as possible on pretend trips—to distract and draw fire from my parents' bitterness, ease my relatives' depressions, escape my own terror. Acting in prescribed roles seemed to contain all the extra pieces of misshapen me. I needed to lose myself in roles until I could find myself in real life.

Trying to get inside that television cabinet with all the hot tubes and wires so my father would delight in me instead of ball games, I finally got there the long way around. I was cast on a comedy show on one of only three existing channels in the early eighties. Our cast of funny unknowns went from anonymity to noticeability fast. The demarcation was clear.

A girlfriend invited me to an event in early fall, when I was on the verge of becoming a known entity in LA, and an attractive guy joined our coterie. I made it clear I wanted to talk to him with excessive body language. He was a man of letters and intellect. I knew I was fated to marry him if he'd only take the hint and I could color my end of our conversation with pithy pronouncements instead of just asides and witticisms.

Noncommittal, he invited me to be a guest at a gathering the following week. I boned up on books, read six *New Yorker* magazines, flexed erudite words while I wrote and rehearsed low comedy for the new TV show. When I arrived at the event, he saw and made a beeline for me, seeming to have lost the alluring unavailability he had the week before.

"I didn't know who you were," he said. "You're funny and you're famous." His eyes glazed over, raising my status, reducing his. It didn't work out.

I played a fake newscaster named after me, just like "Jane Curtin," my castmate from the off-Broadway improv musical troupe The Proposition, did on *SNL*. The words *Melanie Chartoff* were announced while emblazoned on the TV screen and became mnemonically memorable through weekly repetition. My newscaster persona, who covered her irritation with controlled professionalism and was fed jokes written by witty writers, became my go-to default persona in life. No more guessing what people wanted. I could fulfill people's expectations of me with the newscaster's constructed voice and behavior, channeling a few bon mots. From that new ground zero self, I would create

Machiavellian presidents' wives, demented little girls, violent old ladies, and satirized feminist fatales on the show. "Melanie Chartoff" got to be the girl du jour for a while, invited by many talking heads of the time to chat on nighttime, daytime, and early morning talk shows.

It was strange becoming a celebrity, this byproduct of my hunger to disappear into roles and stories worth telling, with fans now aflutter around me while I was aflutter around other inspiring actors. I'd always prided myself on being down-to-earth, unpretentious with long skirts, messy hair, and no makeup, till I was reprimanded by film producer friend, Joel Silver.

"Whassamattuh with you? You can't run around like some little New York stage actress anymore. Wear some makeup. Get your hair styled, for chrissakes. Get some goddamned grown-up clothes!"

His gruffness irked me until he explained he was thinking about my future. He urged me to play the game instead of staying a blank page for repertory theater directors to paint upon. He wanted me to play myself up and get bigger than life-size. Unlike my father, he wanted me to be seen and heard. I made the choice to crank up my charisma, my body language, vocal projection, sex appeal to stand out from the crowd. I realized I could turn it on or off, depending on whether I wanted to shine or disappear that day, to lead or follow. My improvised life could feature different aspects of me every day.

He introduced me to owners of some of the finest stores and designers in Los Angeles and told me I'd better wear tasty stuff when we appeared in public. So I learned to stop satirizing glamour and start cultivating it. I wore the pushup, the strapless, the false, learned to be uncomfortable for a few hours a night.

Rotating the few good investment clothes I owned and was given by designers, I never got televised twice in the same thing. Joel said these machinations were the price I needed to pay to even get thought of for roles, and I'd have to get those roles to afford more glamourous clothes. Talent and luck would have to do the rest, and sometimes the combined factors led to triumphs.

But not my first time on Johnny Carson's *Tonight Show*. My William Morris agents, a pack of cute young Jewish guys, were like new fathers pacing the maternity ward in my dressing room— anxious, encouraging, cautioning. I went to the john to get away from them, thinking only of my father in his BarcaLounger and my mother on her couch awaiting me with Johnny on their home set. This was big.

I'd bought a green $atin dre$$, green crocodile $pike$, had makeup troweled on, and had my hair shaped and teased. I rehearsed an array of answers I'd give from the trial questioning the producer had conducted. I cowered behind the curtain as Doc Severinsen trumpeted me on to hyped applause. I teetered my way in my pretty shoes across the stage as Johnny and Ed McMahon rose like giants to welcome me, as I'd watched them do with hundreds of notables for years. Soon as I sat in the famous hot seat and Johnny made eye contact with me, I felt like I was looking at Mount Rushmore, so etched into my consciousness was Johnny's handsome orange visage. I somehow got through it, faking casual and comfortable, although I saw my behavior as aberrant when I watched it later. I couldn't believe he invited me to come back and that people actually clapped.

I was polite as my battalion of agents walked me to my car in Guest Star parking. I got into my funky Chevy Vega, rushing to make a smooth getaway, and instead of putting it in reverse,

I gunned it forward and smashed the yellow bollards in front of my spot. The guys ran over. I waved them away, gunned it, and rammed the bollards again.

Laughing madly, I cranked down the window. "I'm just fine! Getting a new car anyway!" and finally got the hell out of there with big yellow paint-festooned dents broadcasting my recklessness to other drivers.

My reps said it was urgent that I do Johnny's bidding again soon, and they would drive me next time. For them this was a career triumph, while the split inside my body was engulfing me. But since I had no consultants for a real life, I played out this fake one, as I couldn't live with my inner demons if I didn't. My only choice was do it and suffer or don't and suffer even worse. That's how lost I was, plastering a choice antithetical to my feeling over a fear of alternatives.

Again, I sat and recited preplanned bits to Johnny, then later played my version of Nancy Reagan to his Ronnie. The only personal positive from all this was that my father was big-time thrilled. If I was in good with Johnny, I was in great with him. And even with his approval, my disapproval disease festered inside me. Clearly killing Daddy would have done me no good.

Ironically, my entire cache of glamour gear was stolen from the Vega while it was parked en route to a charity event the following year. I had to start investing and shopping all over again. Wish somebody had stolen the Vega, too.

Despite my desire to embody everybody but me, I landed the bigger-than-life role of "Melanie Chartoff" and began to embody it everywhere. I didn't intend to get famous. I just needed enough people to outvote my internalized negative father so I could believe in myself. Then, it turned out, I would need a lot more people voting to make a secure living and remain in Los Angeles.

Celebrity had its advantages. I liked it when the shoe sales-man greeted me by name and fussed over my feet like old friends. I liked when I called to pay a bill and the operator, recognizing my voice and name, said how much she was affected by some-thing I'd done. I liked the free airfare on the *MGM Grand*, the *Orient Express* of airplanes; the top-drawer hotels; free athletic shoes; and designer outfits. I liked the free daytime parking at William Morris Agency so I could gawk through the Beverly Hills stores for hours. It was like having rich parents.

Not all the free trips were smooth sailing, though. In the ear-ly eighties, I was invited to the Cannes Film Festival to promote a film. Because I was not rich, just suddenly famous, reporter Robin Leach arranged for me to take my first trip to Paris for free, in exchange for staying in a swanky new hotel on the Champs-Élysées and making many mentions of its name, which I've since blocked out. I was given a round sultan's suite of a hot-pink pent-house with a 300-degree view of the city from its balcony. It had a king-size round bed and mirrored ceilings, with murals of erotic female nudes on every wall. Clearly meant for a chieftain and his harem, there were three enormous bathrooms with two bidets each, with lap-pool-size tubs. It was way too much for me—I was used to cozy rooms and beds—and I was promptly moved to a princess room with child-size beds and doll-size dressers, like a little girl's lavender dream room, which suited me far better.

In the mid-eighties my press agent, Sue, and I were invited to the grand opening of El Presidente Hotel and Discoteca in Ensenada, Mexico, along with movie star Mr. James Coburn, sitcom star Mr. Norman Fell, and their assorted entourages. We knew the deal. With all our expenses prepaid, it was understood it would be open season to photograph us anytime we stepped outside our rooms. We were to pose with local dignitaries against photogenic vistas of the hotel, laughing uproariously. Having come from an impoverished family, materially and emotionally, trading on fame had gotten me to some amazing places so far, so I was game.

We landed on an Ensenada tarmac, with fresh tar sucking at our sandals as the desert horizon simmered in unnerving 110-degree heat. Grouchy, we all dashed to the newly built airport lounge to grab our bags. It seemed some sort of drug deal had just gone down, as thugs were being handcuffed by the *policía* at baggage claim and dragged away.

We were shuttled the hell out of there fast, then driven by rattletrap bus with a loud fan through an hour of desolate desert plains, studded with cacti and occasional gravesites with makeshift plastic crucifixes. Actual steer skulls graced the sands between small adobe homes and huts. When we finally arrived at the shimmering oasis of modernity, the still under construction luxury El Presidente Hotel and Discoteca, we dashed fast as we could into the lobby, which had no air conditioning and only one registrar. In his best English, the registrar encouraged us to dip a toe in the *piscina*, which sounded like exactly what it was—a pool the temperature of piss. It would have required two tons of ice cubes to be at all refreshing. We were instructed by the sexy English-speaking lifeguard at the unoccupied pool to avoid the ocean, as there was a man o' war jellyfish infestation lurking in big blobs offshore. One little sting could stun, then kill. We fled to our modern luxury suites to crank up the cool till the 6:00 p.m. grand opening of the El Presidente *restaurante*.

After naps, Sue and I slipped into cocktail dresses and went down to dinner, where we were introduced to all the pretty Miss Mexicos from the different regions. One of them sang the anthem "New York, New York" ("Nueva York, Nueva York") with great gusto, accompanied by a sombrero-wearing mariachi band. We all grinned hard for photos together, but chat was limited as the Miss Mexicos, James Coburn, and Norman Fell had little in common, even those of us who spoke English. Still, we all posed like family, like we hung out in glamorous famous-land all the time, partying behind TV and movie screens. We cracked up together as we ripped the few paper napkins in half. The waitstaff (who had by day been the bellboys, the lifeguard, and maid) were short on supplies. Then we were served many crisp Mexican hors d'oeuvres and ceviche before a main course of spiciness with a side of fish, followed by tropical fruit ice creams and Dom Pérignon.

At nine o'clock it was time to christen the Presidente's *discoteca*. Apparently *el presidente* couldn't make it that night, so I was escorted by Mario, Mexico's minister of tourism. I cut the ribbon to the entrance, under our names on the neon marquee, and people cheered my dexterity with big scissors.

Mario was tall and gracious and showed me all the special features of the grand dance hall, whose sound system was deafening. MTV-style candid films of us celebs getting our bags at the airport pulsed to rock 'n roll hits all evening, making the floors pulse, the walls pulse, our heads pulse. Footage of Coburn's agent procuring and snorting cocaine was prominent, until the agent threatened to sue and that film was quickly taken down.

Mario really liked to dance and liked to dance with me. As the evening wore on, the drunker he got, the more he liked to spin me in my red slit Norma Kamali skirt till it kicked up my thighs, then dip me—faster and faster and lower and lower. After a few too many flings, certain my cranium would soon adorn the floor, I mimed "dizzy" and "need to sit."

I sat and panted at my table with Sue. We cased his moves. He let a few tunes go by, a few drinks go by, then rose and staggered gallantly from his table to approach mine. He bowed once more, only deeper. I smiled, demurred with a fatigued face, told Sue to tell him in her best Spanish that I was simply too tired. He smiled, less graciously, clicked his heels, and withdrew. But I could see him sipping, summoning his grace for one more approach. I tensed. Sue cracked that there could be an international incident if I didn't comply. I risked it, making a beeline for the *baño de mujeres*, then slipped away through the oven of air to my room, to sleep through the night and hide till we were permitted to leave on Sunday. We all showed up at the shuttle at the crack of dawn to get the hell out of there.

I didn't like it when I got followed home from the studio after our late-night parties. I'd stop in front of the 7-Eleven on Sunset Boulevard and ask the friendly neighborhood hooker if I was being tailed.

"Honey, you okay tonight—go 'head home. Nice tights, by the way."

I didn't like some prankster's fabricated Wikipedia entry: "As a teenager, Melanie seduced her stepfather and bore her own stepbrother. She also contracted AIDS from their relationship." It took a while to get that taken down. I didn't like it when an attorney got my home address from the DMV. He showed up on my stoop with flowers, a dossier of his many successful suits against Bob's Big Boy and demands for a dinner date. I had to threaten to get him disbarred to stop his badmouthing me in the tabloids.

I didn't like that I could never tell if someone was befriending me or befriending some trumped-up distortion of me. Did people look twice because they thought I was pretty, or just pretty familiar from the tube? Would anyone ever love the mere me? Would I? In all honesty, I wasn't sure I myself could ever sincerely love someone very famous, who was larger and richer than myself, no matter how talented. I felt the taint of fame would contaminate the purity of interest on both sides. It would be hard to feel attuned. I felt I'd always feel less than.

I felt intimidated by other stars' interest in getting closer—mind-boggled that some bigger-than-life name would know my little one, would muster up more respect for me than my father had been able to express. I feared that these new fair-weather friends would be fickle like my family—with me when I performed perfectly, then otherwise down on or, worse, oblivious to me.

I remember being called back by a casting director to improvise a scene with Robert De Niro in a screen test for Martin Scorsese. As I waited outside their office, the imbalance of power was so throttling me that I couldn't feel my talent, and I got enraged at my inner assassins, my father, at the parochial school dropouts who beat me up and stalked me in high school.

"Screw you, assholes, for making me feel small!" I railed all the expletives under my breath.

"Hi," De Niro said. He'd emerged and was extending a hand. "I'm Robert."

"So wonderful to meet you," I beamed, mirth bubbling up as I stared down my demons on his face and felt fine.

"C'mon in," he said affably. Nice darn guy. I followed him in, saying a continuous, silent "fuck you" at his back under my breath. He had absolutely no idea. My rage at the power some bullies misused carried me through meeting sweet, unimposing Martin Scorsese and doing a scene from *The King of Comedy* in which my character, ultimately played to perfection by Sandra Bernhard in the film, shoves Rupert Pupkin aggressively around. Thereafter, I began thinking in expletives every time I entered a daunting situation. I had to feel that kind of fury to counter the stains of disdain on my soul, to level the playing field.

Getting a VIP pass to meet Pat Metheny after a concert had me trembling with my big crush. When he turned to face me, it was like the moment in *E.T.* when Elliott and the alien see each other for the first time. Two pairs of eyes widened

"You've been the music behind my spiritual journey for years," I squeaked.

"You've made me laugh at the downest times." He grinned back.

Thrilling. Sweet.

The mega-talent Betty Buckley—whom I'd encouraged to be silly in my improv classes, who encouraged my right to sing sad songs in her voice classes, who'd soared to theater, cinematic, and television stardom—had arranged house seats for me to see her premiere on Broadway in *Cats*. My friend Paul and I were barreling down Seventh Avenue to make the curtain. As we approached the Winter Garden, photographers' bulbs were flashing explosively, fighting for the lens meat of big prey stepping out of stretch limos onto the red carpet. We ducked into a souvenir shop entryway. I took off my coat and sneakers and mounted up on green alligator spike heels for the final stagger into the theater.

As soon as we stepped into the limelight, photographers yelled to me to aim my face their way, adding me to the pantheon of collectible images from that night. Despite being acknowledged and greeted by many, I felt like an imposter, an interloper who had snuck into the throngs of the truly accomplished. As we hushed to watch the show, I was too aware of the notables from all the arts, the heady circumstances into which I'd dropped. I drifted in and out; my concentration waned.

Then Betty stepped into a pool of light in the vast dark to sing Grizabella's "Memory." Her command was absolute. Programs did not rustle; bodies did not move. She mainlined feelings into us; her modulation into the final chorus swooped us deep into a sad stray cat's story. Tears swelled and stung a thousand eyelids. Devoid of ego or any sense of separation, we were all just one big emotion in a variety of bodies, entering a natural world of unobstructed human empathy. I knew it was all inside me, too—like other humans who voyaged in the highest realms of the arts. If I could I hang onto this glimpse of my truth within this high-stakes, confusing new world, I might access my authentic self in the rest of it, too.

I tasted fame when millions of viewers were funneled into only three channels, when every program was an event, then again on a fourth network, then on a cable TV hit, but soon there were countless outlets and more series and more overnight sensations to tout. And there were major big screen movie stars outshining us small screen series regulars for lead roles on television as the dearth of good roles for grown-up women became painfully clear.

I recall boarding a flight to Los Angeles, entering through the first-class cabin and seeing Richard Belzer, whom I'd known when I played small clubs in NYC, and who now starred on *Law and Order*. He greeted me warmly, confused that I wasn't settling down near him. But by now I was flying coach again on my own dime, a mere passerby through his compartment of current success.

One night, I dropped into the Los Angeles Improv Club to say hello to old friends. A cute besuited guy stared at me, then made a determined beeline, hand extended. Did he find the real me attractive? Did my persona's past performances change his life? He looked like he thought he knew me well. I extended my paw, racking my brain to recall who the hell this was. And it hung there in the air as he passed me right by to pump the hand of a hot new comedienne. It was her turn. It became more common that people seemed to recognize me, but rather than their gazes snagging on my familiarity, they looked beyond me.

My luminosity began to fade after more than twenty years of getting comfy with it. My voice became a regular on an iconic animated series called *Rugrats* while my younger face lived on in reruns, videos, and DVDs. I was aging out of fashion, out of the passion for youth. Fan mail dwindled; offers tapered off. I wasn't built for the small, exposition bearing roles, just as I'd never fit in the chorus in musicals. I was suited for ensemble character roles, quirky cameo turns, co-leads. While I waited them out, I started writing instead—inventing interesting roles for women in plays, musicals, stories, and screenplays.

I didn't set out to get fame. I was very driven to express my talents with talented others. To play full-out and get the ball returned. As a result, I grow richer every year with very gifted friends whom I love in my life, and with rerun money in the bank. I still learn and teach the craft I developed in decades of improvisation and in my mentor Harry Mastrogeorge's acting classes whenever I'm free. And as I mature, conjuring feelings and translating them in improvisational writing satisfies my hunger for self-expression. Ideas dance in my mind and demand that I grow in my skills and energies to get them heard.

As I worry less about how I appear to others, I've gotten to know and be known for myself.

UNMOTHER'S DAY

I was her first babysitter. She was six weeks old when filmmaker friends entrusted their most precious project to me.

They were torn at taking time away. They had a meeting they had to make. I pooh-poohed their concerns. I oozed faith as they fled out the door. Carmella had foisted emergency numbers, refrigerated breast milk, noisy toys, and her new mother's guilt on me. She had not given me the most crucial things.

I lacked motherly instincts.

In my mid-thirties, I was stunned by feminist friends—turncoats surrendering to men's seeds and needs. I'd not yet yearned to be a mother, although, as an actor, I played them on television. This had to be in my range. I had a womb. I had breasts. I knew the adjectives. I could look the part. The outside could give me the inside. Many had been mothers. We all had one.

My mother was a lousy role model, shocked by others' bodily functions, their weaknesses and needs. I watched her recoil when changing my sister's diapers. I saw her repulsed when I had a rash. I felt her falsity when she visited my father in the hospital. Her squeamishness was larger than her love. I feared the mother thing had maybe skipped me.

But I would not emulate her this day. I drew myself up to my fullest maturity. I reached deep for the right stuff. I took a slug of Carmella's breast milk and nearly retched. I had no taste for mother's milk.

I plopped down on the baby blanket so nothing Lulu did would escape me. I watched her like TV. I was nervous. I'd last babysat when I was fourteen, and then just for the money. Sure, I liked that kid, and his parents were lovely, and they had a nice house on the Connecticut shore, but I was a kid myself. I'd not been trained to actually care for another in the heart sense of the word. I could care only in the physical sense of the word. My attentions wanted to be elsewhere. My affections were nowhere.

Just then, little Lulu's sleeping brow furrowed. A lot seemed to be happening under the surface, in shudders and wiggles. I watched with timid fascination as she took a squinty-eyelid taste of the morning light streaming through the apartment window, disliked it, retreated. Then she peeked with two eyes, blinked a bit, moved her head, scrunched up her face as if smelling something unpleasant. Every move was so darned cute, yet not contrived for effect. I gave her a preemptive pat on her little leg, just below her pink onesie. It didn't seem to register amid all the other stimuli, but, undeterred, I lifted my face within range of hers and grinned her a goofy "Hi, Lulu!"

I thought I detected a Borscht Belt double take from her little face, but who would have taught her that? She was just two months old, she wasn't yet in show biz, and she wasn't even Jewish. Her activated little body wrinkled the yellow storks and bunnies on the baby blanket beneath her. Little nonsense sounds emitted from her throat. I don't recall ever seeing something human be so adorable. I prolonged another "Hiiiii!" and added a finger wave near her face.

She focused fully on my finger for a second. The next thing

that came into her eyes was my involuntarily beaming face. Her eyes rounded. I could only describe her facial expression as amazed. And then, the international expression we'd all call joy ray-gunned into my shy eyes and warmed them confident. Touched, I welcomed her into my face with another "Hi, Lulu!" and a chortle erupted out of her.

Wow. This wasn't even my A material.

"Hiiiiiii!" I squealed like a maniac.

A pause. A subliminal decision. Then, she cracked up in an ongoing chuckle. I cracked up, too. I never knew how ecstatic laughing into a baby's eyes could be. I sucked an unfamiliar openness from hers. She didn't avert; she had no time limit. She had no compunctions about staring, smiling at length into my face.

I fed her with pleasure, and I changed her with tenderness. Connect Velcro tab A to part B—it was illustrated on the label. She was better than paper dolls, better than stuffed animals ever were. I lay her down for a nap and watched her drop into sleep with a sappy, silly love welling up in me.

I babysat her as much as they'd let me in months to come. Watching her transition into sleep or wakefulness became my favorite pastime. Her face was my favorite film. I was there when she cut her first tooth. I was there when she had her first grand mal seizure. I was in the hospital with her mother when Lulu wore a headdress of electrodes for a supervised sleep. I watched with her father as the monitor graph grew black with squiggly lines as she seized and seized again. Her sleep became a nightmare from the time she was twelve months old. The Picasso paintings of sleep watchers I had long loved took on a more sinister hue.

I wanted to be there for the special diets, the reading lessons, all that they went through in the years as she grew, until they moved away and I had to grow up and miss her like a big girl. But I'll never forget her. I sucked my first maternal instincts from her eyes. I nursed my notion of selflessness from her arms. Because of her, there was hope for me to love.

I turned thirty-eight, and my biological alarm was clanging. I needed to make a decision. Would I or wouldn't I? I needed a sign. I always thought I would but got distracted by my acting. I got stalled by series deals. I got waylaid in loving and living with an independent filmmaker.

The call to find father material seemed less urgent in me than the call to love him and the call to be on camera, sometimes his camera. I thought parental desire might overcome ambition as we grew more successful, but our projects were our babies, our careers our pride and joy, our movies our immortality. We felt too infertile and too un-forever for a real-life family.

But I loved babysitting Alex, his sister Anne's infant. The first time we were alone, I watched, undaunted, like I watched Lulu, this bundle of nothing but needs napping on his baby blanket. I knew so much more about babies now, having held and smelled so many in recent years. I was now especially focused on that tenuous moment when they'd first awaken.

Alex showed no signs of abnormal sleep patterns. I knew he was a balanced baby, and his waking could go either way—glad or mad, regardless of who was at the helm.

As Alex surfaced, I came closer and hummed "Blackbird." He erupted awake, teetered like a silent movie star making every face known to humankind, recognized me, then broke into a smile that mainlined delight into my heart. I got goofy and giggly, and I noticed I got longing.

As months passed, Alex liked me to tuck him in when I was

there. We deemed me Auntie. We bonded. I loved his innocence. I could do the same material over and over and over. He never seemed to get that no matter how many times we played peekaboo, I would always be there behind our hands.

I read him bedtime stories. I played all the parts. He chortled and mimicked me. His appreciation was worth all my silly character voices and goofy playacting. I made a fool of myself for him like for no other man. He trusted me; he took my hand very confidently as a toddler on some of his first swaggers. His trust enlarged me.

One day Anne called me freaked from work. Alex had fallen into the coffee table and split his top lip open. The nanny was unable to calm him. Could I get there until she could?

I dropped everything. I rocketed to her house a mile away. The bloodied nanny let me in. We ran to his side on the kitchen floor. His screams were splitting his lip wider and wider. Blood and tears were pouring all over. *Oh, God,* came to my mind, and I didn't even believe in God that I knew of. I took him kicking and inconsolable into my arms, as the nanny grabbed ice cubes from the freezer in a cloth to hold to his mouth. He shoved her hand away. He didn't recognize my peekaboo eyes or Auntie face. I hummed and held him to my heart. He flailed; he kicked. His eyes grew wild like an animal in captivity; his primitive shrieks grew shrill.

Then, suddenly, he stopped.

I thought my love had calmed him. I thought my arms were comforting him. I hoped that his wound might not worsen on my watch. I was semi-aware of his baby blood dripping down his *Toy Story* T-shirt onto my shaky arms and the yellow linoleum floor in the too-sunny suburban kitchen. I noticed the little Guatemalan nanny had dropped the ice cubes onto the kitchen throw rug. She seemed to be in a trance, gazing over my shoulder, maybe longing for her own children too many countries and dollars away. I could hear the dog barking and whining in the attached garage.

Then it hit me, and I turned.

Anne had come into the kitchen, car keys clenched in her fist, and behind me she was reaching for him. Tears of remorse were streaming down her cheeks. I'd driven fast, but I knew, racing here from Hollywood, she had driven far faster.

I was transfixed. I was humbled by the look that passed between them. I surrendered Alex to her arms, the strength and faith in her face. He knew everything would be all right now. As the nanny gathered a blanket to him, I was flooded with relief, tenderness, helplessness, plus an acid drip of shame and envy. What the hell was that about?

"Will you drive us to the hospital?" Anne asked, throwing me the keys.

I held his foot as they butterfly bandaged up his mouth, as the doctor reassured Anne that, if there were a scar, it would give his baby face character. Anne and I were giddy at the diagnosis. Alex was quiet. He seemed in a state of grace, gazing at Anne. Alex never shed a tear the whole time.

But I was sad inside because now I knew for sure: as close as I might come as the sitter, the helper, the auntie, the third lap from the source, I could never be the necessary, the integral entity. I would never be the portal for a life to be born. I would never be the one a baby knew would make everything all right—the everyday heroine who'd sacrifice her white business suit, her job, her dignity, her safety, her life to make him safe. I would never choose to be fully responsible. For me, too much could go wrong to risk the right. I would never be a mother.

THE MESSAGE

I listen to my mother's message on my answering machine from the stage phone while on a break from rehearsing a new series. She never called me, so I know something is up.

Her voice sounds tight, tense. *What'd I do now,* I'm thinking, but go out to a pay phone to reach her at the unfamiliar Connecticut number.

"I have some things to tell you," she says.

"Really? What?" I'm crunching on celery from craft services' table of treats. The crew food featured sugary and starchy snacks—bagels, cheese, and donuts—with a small concession to us fussy actors at the end of the table: obligatory vegetables in crudité form, fruit, rice cakes, and a few packaged dips and powdered soups.

"Well, I'm singing a solo with my new choir on Mother's Day, for one thing."

"That's great, Mom. I think I can come east then. Where will it be?"

"At Woolsey Hall at Yale," she says.

'Wow—big-time! I cannot wait to see you up there." I'm chewing subtly as I can.

"My driving is going great now. The therapy really helped, and the driving lessons, too."

"Proud of you—back on the horse, right?"

"Yup. And . . . "

"Gotta go. And?"

"I'm leaving your father."

I held my breath a very long time before emitting a dumfounded "Huh?"

"I've got a good attorney, a secret place to stay. The time is right."

"Mom!" A wad of celery string falls out of my mouth.

"I borrowed a couple suitcases, put 'em in my car trunk. I've been putting things out there for weeks, leaving dummy clothes in the closets."

"You've planned this all out."

"I'll keep you and Norma out of it. I don't want you involved or blamed. But I'll be going underground for a while, staying in a secret apartment in New Haven, so he may need you two at the beginning."

"When?"

She speaks in low tones. "He's going in for gall bladder removal Monday. I'll explain everything in a letter and have the nurse give it to him after the surgery. That way if he reads it and has a heart attack, he's already in the hospital."

"Wow."

"I've dreamed about leaving, but it was always just make-believe. Remember when you and Norma ran away from home and I went with you? Then you missed your teachers, so we came back? I didn't want to, but we had no money, no place to go."

"I remember." I'm excited for her and me and my sister, too. "It's about time."

"You're not mad?"

"I don't know how you endured this whole opera between you this long."

"People married for life in our day. And he supported us and drove us around and put up with me."

"He put up with *you*?!"

"If only you hadn't moved so far away."

"I couldn't stand the way he talked to us, especially to you."

"You know, I feel like you and Hal fighting was mostly my fault."

"Hey. I had my own issues. His chauvinism made me a women's libber by the time I was twelve."

"A woman's liver. That's what I want to be— a woman who lives for herself . . . "

"All his yelling made me fight for independence. And now you're going to get some, too," I said.

She sounds nervous. "Yes, I guess I am."

"So brave! At last!"

"I feel like I've been living dead all these years. But I'm planning on dying alive."

I'm feeling teary, apprehensive for her.

"Know what? You are becoming the mother we always wanted."

"I hope so, dear."

"I love you very much. I'll call you later—where?"

"I can't give this number out. I'll call you."

"Oh," I say, amazed by the intrigue, yet nervous about her inaccessibility. My little baby mother is leaving home. I choke up like she's graduating from college. "Take care, okay?"

And she clicks off.

I rush back to the stage, fighting tears. What an astonishing turn of events. After forty-two years of melodrama between them—this! Maybe I don't have to feel guilty about my life anymore, about my every success being an assault on her lack. Maybe now that she, a chooser of losers, is getting rid of hers, this meant I can choose a loving forever husband and marriage without feeling like I was flaunting it. My little mother is finally growing up and finding a new haven in herself at the age of sixty-five. Maybe when I'm sixty-five there'll be hope for me.

THE BARRENNESS

It takes more muscles to smile; I defy gravity to laugh. There's more time between my full moons. I am losing the glow of youth, shedding enough hair in my hairbrush each day to make a merkin for when my hair down there goes, too. Listless, restless, sexless—I am officially infertile.

I circled the surgeon's office, assessed his many plaques from women's organizations, a framed shot of the wife and two daughters smiling, secure with Daddy looming large around them and Machu Picchu looming large around him. I approached my X-rays on the screen—a Rorschach in shades of gray—an ultrasound of my alleged ovaries.

Peals of laughter welcomed his voice in the hallway. All the women who work and visit here adore him. He's a nice, modern, post-feminist metrosexual. Swooshing in, smelling of soap, he allotted me one professional smile, then addressed my smudge on his screen, pointing to what he suggests is my right ovary enveloped by a benign growth, then to my left one, also "at risk." He said that one's got to go, and while he's in there, he might as well take this one and the rest of my reproductive system, too.

I was stunned. He explained to my dropped-jawed face: he'd come in through the navel, snip-snip, scar free, and remove all the useless stuff.

"Stuff?! You mean the stuff that makes me female, makes me *me*, stuff?" I asked.

Yes, Mr. Trigger-Happy wants every vestigial thing not in current use out out out. He'll probably bill my insurance company extra so he can fly the juicy wife and girls to Bali on the back of my ovaries, cervix, and fallopian tubes.

"Hey, hey," he said gently. "Go think about it. Get a second opinion, do your research, but decide soon. Don't invite trouble. You're over fifty—what do you need with all that?"

He made my womb sound like a toxic dump. How could he be so casual about ripping my guts out, performing a gender cleansing? Was I just another opportunity for him to show off his dissecting skills for interns?

Aghast, clutching my purse and all my precious pulps to the middle of me, I spun in his doorway and said, too loudly for an office, "Find yourself another practice round, another crash dummy, you ageist, sexist butcher!"

Ploughing past the cheery females at the front desk, I grabbed the women's room key, a shuttlecock with a ruler attached. *What the hell does that signify?* My seething exit left all these Beverly Hills lemmings—these sheep, these Bedford Drive wives—in his waiting room alarmed at my outburst, not to mention the disappearance of the bathroom key.

I sniffled in the sanctuary of my car, stashing the shuttlecock key as a hostage under my seat. It's like *Invasion of the Body Snatchers* here. All my neighbors going under the knife—no one has original parts or faces or even thoughts. Traffic stalled my cinematic getaway from the valet.

I suppressed a scream, worrying. *I've got to get out of this vanity state with its vanity plates, with its stenciled expressions on platypus-lipped, cookie-cutter faces. Isn't a full hysterectomy over-kill? and why isn't it a "hers-terectomy"? Why is everything his!? Wouldn't the upper parts of me collapse without these placehold-ers? Would my breasts fall onto my stomach, my intestines onto my bladder?*

Safe at home, I cogitated.

I'll escape—that's what I'll do. I'll move to another planet—like Animal Planet, only this will be the Women Who Have No Surgeries Planet. Pretty soon this whole galaxy will be colonized like cable TV: the Porn Planet, Life in Prison Planet, Addiction-Recovery Planet, Retirement Planet, the Religion Planet, the Landfill Planet. I'll colonize a planet for Women Who Age As Is. There, with our faces relaxed and swinging, we'll galumph around, our rounded bellies like cowcatchers moving the underbrush aside, as we gather fatty foods in our soft, comfy muumuus. This way, young earthlings won't have to look at us harbingers of their own time-release decrepitude, the birth of their own deaths. This way, we elders can relax, cackling, wrinkling, our restless breasts re-leased, upper-arm skin like angels' wings flapping in the breeze, our geisha feet finally spreading, free of the spiked heels invented by diabolical men to handicap us. There we can all sag and spread without shame among our own.

They took my tonsils when I was a kid, but they were infected. My wisdom teeth pained me, too—they were taken in my teens. But my ovaries and tubes didn't hurt. I'd hardly have known they were there if I hadn't seen photos, which were maybe faked, like the walk on the moon. These parts still held the sentimental mag-ic of the motherhood I'd missed. Didn't I need them all to be a complete woman? Maybe sexuality is all in the mind, but isn't it down there, too?

I did my due diligence, sought second opinions. My female gynecologist concurred with Dr. Trigger-Happy, as did my lesbian gastroenterologist and my female cardiologist, a mother of three. These turncoats said they wished they had an excuse to get theirs out, too. Women's innards seemed to have this time bomb-type reputation. Why, they could explode at any moment, like landmines—like live grenades, with our bodies thrown over them. These denatured women were so duped by the patriarchal medical establishment, anticipating decay at every turn, they couldn't be objective. I consulted with prior patients of the doctor.

"Oh, do it—he's witty, wonderful. It was like being on a date," said one.

"Compared to my cesareans, it was like nothing," said another. "Like a vacation. I was pampered by my family, rested, and back at the gym in two days—and best of all, I lost a pound!"

Of course, this was from women who'd already dropped their foals in the open fields of Beverly Hills. Women who'd had several kids, cesareans, and belly lifts, who were accustomed to having their bodies ripped apart on a regular basis.

"Look, my uterus served its purpose. It got me the husband and the kids. What does it matter now that it's over fifty?"

Evidence was mounting against me. Still, my inner voice yelled no. I decided I would take six months to conduct further research and dislodge this thing by natural means: visualizing Pac-Man chomping it away, trampolining, cartwheeling, hanging upside down from the trapeze. Then it occurred to me that there might be other means of shaking this cyst from my system.

I had been a wholesome virgin in the Free Love sixties, when everyone else was having wild, unbridled sex. After I was deflowered, I become serially monogamous. I could count the men I'd had sex with on two hands—all white, all older and a little taller. Why, it would be small-minded of me to stop there! I decided to explore my libido with different men—take a crash course—different ages, colors, sizes, types, astrological signs. I'd make up for lost time. I'd up the estrogen and testosterone allotted to me on menopause and ignite my lust, put myself in heat. Yes! Before I got spayed, I'd get myself thoroughly, vigorously, exploratorily laid. I'd be the barren, wanton baroness of Beverly Hills.

I was honest—the nice men I approached through work and social events knew I only wanted one thing, knew there was no risk of pregnancy or STDs. I carried proof at all times, plus a confidentiality agreement. When I told them it was a medical necessity, most were more than happy to help. First, a Black guy half my age, with hair twice as long; next, a tattooed heavy metal rock star who came with his own MTV video; one a Portuguese car dealer who threw in a tune-up for free; another a short stunt actor who compensated for his small stature with incredible speed. I was so overdosed on testosterone I was a walking erogenous zone. And I definitely had more balls than ever before. I was so hot that if a nice man simply said hello or smiled at me in the elevator, I'd react.

"Hey, buddy—watch out. Y'know you're askin' for it? You'll give me blue vagina, you big tease." And if he smiled one more time, "Okay. That's it. Let's go!" I'd be ready to take him right there between floors. It didn't take much. Oh, maybe I was infertile, but I had never been so hot to trot. It was a blur, this half year of easy travel to other worlds, with no passports, no shots, no baggage, no dreary talk of marriage or of love.

But, alas, when my six months were up, a third opinion reported the cyst was now larger. And the mounting din of statistics did not favor strolling along any more holistic pathways, musing in creative visualizations. My efforts, though educational and very, very entertaining, had been futile. The body of evidence asserted that we females were born burdened with more parts with more pain and problems with those parts. Time to grieve and get perspective.

I'll never have kids, I wallowed, tossing used tissue turds around my bed. *But I will have art, dance, theater, music, comedy. I'll have aloneness and self-absorption, but with artistic freedom. There'll be no accidental pregnancies, no abortions, no child to screw up with my own problems. I'll go to foreign movies and museums and retreats while friends with kids watch the Disney Channel and childproof their homes in pastels.*

I'll have magazines, memberships, classes, charities, projects, a guppy, a puppy, no stretch marks, and a fertile imagination with too many ideas to nurture to even think about kids. I'll have self-improvement and sleepless nights for lots of other reasons. I'll justify my life, my value in other ways yet to be discovered. I'll send up flares for a broken-in single father with a prefab family.

Clearer-minded, freer of the madness of fertility, an older, wiser barrenness returned to Dr. Trigger-Happy. He agreed to take just the one cystic ovary in exchange for yearly ultrasounds. And he graciously welcomed back the shuttlecock key, no questions asked.

HAPPILY NEVER AFTER

"**M**y mother and father are divorced. I'm from a broken home."

I have always wanted to say that and to be that. Now I'm forty-two years old and without married parents, and I could not be happier.

But not for my father.

During that one frantic hour Mom finally packed up her car and fled his home to live with a friend, my unknowing father was at the dentist's office to have a tooth pulled before he checked into the hospital for gall bladder removal and had a stroke in the chair. As he convalesced in the hospital, she visited and left him a Dear John note for the Puerto Rican nurse to read him. Semi-paralyzed, bewildered by her heavy accent, he couldn't get the gist. When I rushed east to relieve my sister, to be with him, I had to explain it fully.

"Daddy. Your wife, my mother, won't be living at your house anymore when you go home."

Mouth agape, he stared. And when it fully landed, half his face fell in as half his mouth screeched, "What?! Are you nuts? She can't get along without me!"

"She wants to try," I said.

Then, his whole body contorted in the hospital bed as full

sensation came cruelly back to him, and I saw my father weep for the first time ever—the tyrant, the tough guy melting like the Wicked Witch of the West into the sheets. I wept along with him, holding his hand tight for what he faced. My sister agreed that she and her husband would get him through. We needed to parent our parents now. It would be hard, but we both felt they'd both be better off apart.

Then my mother fell apart, too.

I'd brought her to Los Angeles to visit. I don't know what I expected. I romanticized our new relationship. I wanted to celebrate her freedom, congratulate her courage, take her on a trip up the California coast, take her to feminist lectures, show her beautiful things, but she sat in the spare room staring into space, day and night. I'd felt her freedom might shift the sands under my own relationship issues. I thought I might now feel okay about loving someone. Maybe now that her horrendous marriage was over, I could embark on a good one. I gave her time but felt frustrated. I wanted a magical miracle mother now. I wanted us to laugh and let go of the past with my father. Mom cocooned for days. Then, playing like I was still her little girl, lying on the guest bed beside her, I begged her for a bedtime story, and she told me one.

"Once upon a time, I fell in love," she said. "With Clark, my boss at the college."

I'd never heard this one before. Her repertoire had consisted of Russian lullabies, Dr. Seuss stories, and sentimental tales of singing opera for the governor of Connecticut when she was twelve.

"While Clark was giving me driving lessons, we went parking, went on picnics, we necked," she said. Wait a minute. This was completely new material. This was real.

"What? Mom, really?" I was stunned to hear that my mother had some happiness, some affection in her life at last. I wanted so much for her. I couldn't even picture my mother being sexual. She seemed above and beyond it, or like she'd forgotten it. I recalled how in the heights of my own sexual passion I'd often feel guilty. *My mother has never had anything like this,* I'd think as I came. *Here's one for Mom,* as I came again.

She stiffened. "The day I left your father, Clark was supposed to meet me at the secret apartment and tell me if would leave his wife."

"Yeah?" *This is what soap operas are like, except starring younger, more beautiful adulterers,* I thought. She petered out. I held my breath.

"Hey. You're not going to just leave me hangin' here, are you?!"

"But he didn't show up."

"Oh, son of a *bitch*," I yelped, pained.

"He had a heart attack and died on the tennis court that same day I left Daddy."

"No! No. No. No."

"So, I'll never ever know if he would have left Clara or not. But"—her eyes teared into mine—"at least I found out what love, what falling in love feels like, for the first time in my whole life. I'm so glad I finally got to feel that."

And now I needed to mourn the death of this brief hope, which she had buried the year before. I had never known my mother happily in love, I'd only known her loveless, like she might be now. I wanted her to feel my love more than ever before.

I cooked her favorite things, we went to bookstores to find her new favorite reads. After a week, she still wasn't eating or getting dressed, just sat staring into space in her unfastened nightie, and I grew more concerned. She was frail. As a child when I saw my mother without her clothes on, her body seemed abnormally exposed, parts that were supposed to be on the inside were on the outside, as though she couldn't contain all the inflamed life inside—blue veins surfaced through her translucent skin, nipples and areola the most naked part of all, calling for attention, her possum clothed in pale gray. I always looked away in embarrassment. I feared there was something wrong with my mother and I might catch it, or maybe there was something wrong with me for feeling revulsed by it. I wanted to look away from her helplessness now. Maybe my shrink would fix her.

On the way to a joint session with my genius-by-the hour therapist, Susan, I took Mom to see the sun setting on the Pacific, nestling slowly into clouds on blue sky and water, rosily pinking us and everything else. I'd always wanted to drive into the sunset with my mother safe by my side. I wanted her to see the world anew through liberated eyes. I sighed happily and looked to the passenger seat, to see her staring down at her hands, at her shrunken fourth finger, denuded of her wedding band at last.

"Mom? Look how pretty it is! It's setting on the ocean. Different than in Connecticut, where it comes up on the ocean," I murmured.

She spun to me with a sneer like the possessed girl in *The Exorcist*, grotesque, snarling, "Leave me alone! I've seen the goddamned sunset before!"

Sudden vitriol snaked up my esophagus, too, and I bit it back and drove us straight to Susan's office to deep dive into the glut of rage now broiling in us both. With her divorce, my long-suppressed disappointment and disrespect of her weakness came unveiled, and so did her rage toward and envy of me.

In several sessions with my therapist in LA and then hers in New Haven, we processed. With the adversary of my father now out of the ring, our gloves came off with each other. First her anger at me for going off to college, then for having a career in New York and Los Angeles, for not saving her and my sister from my father. For not visiting to deflect his blows with my own body and brain more often. Then my rebuke of her for leaving us kids like bait, for never protecting or defending me, my sister, or herself from years of degradation and enfeeblement. For not taking me up on my invite to come live in New York or California. We yelled and wept and simmered and struggled through a year of phone calls and letters.

Then, during one of my visits to her little apartment in Hamden, something cleared.

"I'm sorry," she said.

I looked up from reading the paper. "Oh? For?"

"For your father being so mean to me that I was too scared to take care of you."

I sagged. "Nice try," I said. "Let me know when you can take responsibility for your part."

"What do you mean, my part—what part?"

"The part of you that was separate from him. The separate person that took his side, that let him yell and scream and control us all. That could have stuck up for us and for you."

"Oh," she said, and paused in deep thought. "Uh-huh. I'll get back to you."

I've got to hand it to her. She took a crash course. She crammed, determined. She went to twelve-step meetings for Co-Dependents Anonymous, got more therapy, did yoga, made new, more honest friends, and a year later she called me.

"I'm sorry," she said, with a tremolo, "for everything that happened to you and your sister. Can you forgive me?"

"For?"

"For being weak. For not rescuing you. For letting him slap you and insult you. For not finding a way to get us out of there."

"Yes, Mom," I said. "And I'm sorry I was just a kid without a grown-up part yet and couldn't do anything but save my own life," I said over a brick in my throat. "But I really wanted to."

"Well. Okay," she said.

I wished I could take her hand. "I love you, Mom!"

We understood better and forgave in words. All was not forgotten. We still had knee-jerk and heart-jerk reactions to each other when we were together, but I began to sense what a normal mother-daughter love, free of pity, fear, or the need for protection, free of contempt, resentment, and blame, free of guilt and grief, might feel like. I hoped to hell we'd both live long enough to do the work to get there and love each other for more than moments.

EXTRA HELPINGS

spent the spring of 1995 watching him worsen. I watched the pussy willows out the window of the rest home ripen from green buds to furry little animals. I watched his body waste away and waited for a sign our hearts would soften. I began composing a speech in my mind.

Here lies Harold, born and raised in a delicatessen. Amazing he lived this long, the way he ate—the way he cooked. He never met a vegetable he couldn't render unrecognizable. Cabbage marinated to a mystery. Carrots pickled to oblivion. I never knew how food was really meant to taste till I went away to college. I never knew how love was meant to feel till he welcomed me home.

But he never had, and I never went.

I had deified my handsome daddy when I was little. Then when he outshouted my mother and demeaned my dreams, I defied him and stayed far away—until my sister called for help.

He'd opted for his third triple bypass, and the new hog's valve was hiccupping in his heart. As soon as he got home from the hospital, he knew something wasn't kosher. The organ was chugging arrhythmically along, and the rest of his body couldn't keep the beat or keep up. It was like being dragged behind a horse. He wanted it to end.

"Not because I'm some brave guy," he said. "I just can't see any other way out." There wasn't. Yet he and his stubborn life force fought any evidence of failing.

"This isn't normal," he'd bellow.

"This is normal . . . for dying," the hospice worker assured us. The hospice care made it clear that Dad's descent was irreversible. This was forcing me to rethink every single word and action. Compassion was running neck and neck with bitterness in my psyche. I was rooting hard for compassion to win.

"Dad?"

He surfaced slowly from a fitful sleep, struggling to understand where he was and who the hell I was. Pointless "Get Well" balloons were hovering near the ceiling. Finally, he focused on my face.

"Oh, it's you. You still here?"

"I'm going to your old friend Manny's sandwich shop. Can I get you something?"

"Yeah," he brightened a watt or two. "Get me a ham sandwich, thick-sliced, on rye, with three slices of Swiss cheese, Gulden's mustard, and garlic pickles."

"Sure," I said, grabbing my coat to go.

"And . . . thank you," he said.

He'd not said thank you to me since I'd grown up and away from his entitlement—and never in this way. He was trying, too. This was more than sandwich gratitude, and I was determined to take nourishment from any crumb he offered.

"Well, you are very, very welcome." I smiled.

Driving through the old neighborhood, I put a more positive spin on his eulogy.

How this man could concoct. How this man could create. My dad invented "matzoh-rella marinara," and my sister and I were his "garlic girls," chopping it for hours on end to make batches of his sauce. Our hands stunk so much that even the fishermen's daughters stayed away. We'd spoon layers of that marinara over thick slices of mozzarella on matzohs. And we topped these matzoh pizzas with slices of lamb sausage from the Greeks. On Sundays, neighbors would bring their ethnic dishes over, and Dad would celebrate all the differences in tastes. He was a true "Jewmanist."

Manny made the sandwich and helped me carry an optimistic eight cans of Ensure to the car. He was seventy-three, like Dad, but still fit and feisty.

"He won't drink that crap," Manny said.

"It's the only thing that stays down," I said. "He needs to keep up his strength."

The "For what?" smirk in his eyes made me sad.

For us to love each other! I knew inside.

When I brought him back the sandwich, with romantic notions of atonement on my mind, his drugs were wearing off. He opened his eyes. I opened the bag. He opened the sandwich. He summoned his strength. He raised a furious face to mine.

"Hey! I asked you for the ham thick-sliced!" he growled. Hurt resurfaced and darkened his obituary.

Dad inherited his overeating from Grandpa, dead at sixty-two, and his fat-happy cooking from Grandma, dead at sixty. Aunts, uncles, cousins—one whole branch of his family was wiped out by heart disease. The Holocaust didn't help, but it was the cholesterol that did them in.

The hospice helper took me into a hallway, where dogwood blossoms danced outside the windows. She carried a clipboard with his history.

"It won't be long," she said. "His heart will give out soon. You should call your family."

"There's nobody left to come. He always ate too much and made himself sick and mad. He drove my mother to divorce, and me and my sister away."

"But he did not make himself sick," she corrected.

"What do you mean? He ate like there was no tomorrow."

"There almost wasn't," she said. "It says here Harold got rheumatic fever in the Air Force outbreak in 1943. Those poor guys all suffered severe heart damage. They were doomed. He must've had a strong will and loved you all very much to live this long."

It took me a moment to reframe this—that my tyrannical father had been a victim of his sick ventricles, and so had we all. He'd lived a diminished life in constant fear and pain. And in my resentment and oblivion, I hadn't really considered that. He'd been expecting, dreading this last moment all his life. Returning to his room, I knew I'd better make the most of it.

There I saw the shell of Harold in hell, lying in his last bed. As an aide opened his smock to bathe him, I saw his once beautiful hairy chest slashed with the sign of the cross in three parallel scars across his lapsed Jewish rib cage. My resistance liquidated in sympathy. The rock in my belly was melting. Oh, no. Now I'd have to feel the loss of the first love of my life, damn it. I covered his hand with mine.

He felt my empathy, opened his eyes, softened his focus, and after a moment said, "You know what, kid? I can be a jerk, too."

I wasn't sure if it was Dad, the drugs, or dementia talking, but that sounded oddly like an apology. An apology and a thank-you in the space of an hour? I knew it wouldn't be long now.

"I . . . love you, Daddy," I quavered like his little girl, who'd gone so very far from him, who'd just this moment gotten back.

"Hey. I always loved you, kid," he whispered. "Even when you were mad at me, I always loved you."

He left his damaged, defective body behind like a chrysalis soon after, and his spirit flew pain free. I knew the presence of his absence would stay large in my mind.

And in 1995, on a ridiculously beautiful spring day at the New Haven Jewish Cemetery, I eulogized at his final resting place.

"Dad loved to picnic on this gravesite, with the Jewish star on it, given free for his service in World War II.

'Hey! It's a lovely little piece of property,' he'd say. 'Why wait till I'm dead to enjoy it?'

"He knew loss young, as his whole big deli family left him behind. Their section of this cemetery is so crowded, you've got to take a number to get in.

"He was funny and feisty and always hungry. Food and laughter were the currencies of love my father offered most freely. Our hungers weren't quelled, but he gave us big appetites for as many helpings of life as we could get."

MISSING SISTER

I analyzed. I paced as we spoke, dusted a few knickknacks with a spare hand. I proposed a novel point of view, worded some metaphors rather well. I pontificated about what I assumed had happened with her and our problematic father and awaited her usual agreement.

Voice calls leave so much of the other's response to our imaginations—the nod, the elevated eyebrow of approval, the body language of acquiescence. There was silence on the line. Longer silence. Wait. Was I hearing the grimace of dissent? Nah. That would be new. But as the pregnant pause prolonged, the giggling little sister of yesteryear began to get blurred by her now fifty-year-old face in my fifty-five-year-old mind's eye.

"Don't ever talk to me again," she said and clicked off.

"What?" I said to empty air, trying to milk meaning from the hiss of my portable handset. It remained pressed to my ear. My arm was stuck in space.

"What?" Despite being body-slammed I stayed standing, staring into the yard, blind to the patient old trees, deaf to the daffy bird squawks. Delaying the onset of shock, I clung to our final second of connection and the last dregs of intimacy.

Seconds passed. My face felt numb. My arm tingled. My chest ached. The slant of late-day light in my bedroom was blinding, the sun refracting, rainbowing through a beveled window, ricocheting off my bureau mirror, floating a small green beam down the opposite wall like Tinkerbell. It was dark where she was, three hours ahead, at the eastern edge of the country. There, spring had yet to begin, while here jasmine was perfuming the air. That's how far apart we were—day and night, spring and winter. That's how difficult it would be to take her in my arms to apologize for whatever slight she might have inferred from my words.

Maybe I was just on hold. If I stayed still, maybe she'd pick up again. I'd lurk here till then. Once, with landlines, when someone hung up on you, there was a dial tone of finality—a droning "nooooooo." It used to be, with landlines, that you could hang on after they hung up and they might just pick up again to call you back and you'd be there, ready to welcome them back.

"Still here!"

Those days were over, as lines were going digital and our relationship only long-distance. The phone finally clicked through to a beep-beep-beep, then quiet, and I was alone. I placed the handset in its charger. Phones were pointless devices once emptied of the possibility of connection. My hand was clammy.

I couldn't stand here. I had to do something to ease the stun gun spray of fear heading right for my heart. Calling her back would be disrespectful and weak, emailing too easy and disposable. I had no idea what to even say, as I couldn't recall what I had said or what she might have thought I meant. It was now between me and me. Face the music. But I wasn't sure I should give penance for something I didn't understand. My sister seemed to have inherited the belief from my parents that my neutral acts were endowed with malevolent intent, and a lifetime of defending myself had never altered their interpretations. Could it have been my tone? Maybe I put an edge on whatever innocuous something I said, and now I was getting excommunicated for all time.

For weeks, I avoided reclining, starving myself of sleep. I dreaded the obsessive thoughts that would lurk when I lay down, the replays of I-said-but-she-heard-but-I-meant. For weeks I blurred busy, until, as a last resort, I drugged myself and dropped into sleep that was like a TV outage, the onslaught of images instantly encased in black.

This became my routine. Popping a pill, immersing myself in television until it kicked in. Then, all input ceased, and my face creased into unconsciousness for six hours, tops. Until a slim crack of light broke into my encrusted eye with the incessant drone of CNN injecting bad news into my ear. I'd left it on all night again. I'd step into socks and panties in unaesthetic order, not even looking in the mirror to make sure my colors matched, my usual habit when I liked myself. Now I just pulled a shirt over my head, brassiered beneath its shelter, though no one, not even me, was interested in looking.

Dressed, I skipped past that reorientation when bleak thoughts might come, splashing iciness, gargling mintyness, brushing my teeth brusquely, brushing my hair blindly, diving into action, bleary-eyed, busy-busy with my lists and tasks until pill time.

On my deep-winter birthday eight months later, I checked my front stoop. I searched my mail, twice. My usual card from her was flagrantly absent. I was bereft. A lifelong ritual skipped, its lack a big message. Could that spigot of sweetness between us be stopped up forever? She used to love me. I have pictures. I have letters.

I dug out and reread her card from the prior year that said a simple happy birthday with a picture of two girls smiling conspiratorially. It was signed with the x's and o's of last year's love. It had arrived attached to a bulky object, inside brown paper, taped into kids' toy-type gift wrap. It was my childhood Alice in Wonderland doll, which she had painstakingly reconstructed. She had cleaned the painted wood of Alice's cheeks, washed and ironed the pale-blue skirt and the white apron, detangled the blonde doll hair, elaborately wrapped and ribboned it, and sent it to me last year when she loved me.

What did I say that changed that? Something about our father trying to squash us, never letting us win at wrestling or checkers, never supporting our independence, something about our mother being helpless. Something innocuous that might never have upset her in the past, but now—

I reflected on our childhood, how at age four I had resented her birth, thinking what the hell did they need her for? Didn't I give my parents anything they could ever want from a kid? Maybe she'd somehow unblocked the memory of me touching the forbidden ripe, soft spot at the crown of her baby-peach, still-hardening head when it was three days old. For weeks I'd hide when she cried, fearing that as soon as she could talk, she'd point a finger and yell, "She tried to kill me!" But she soon became my favorite playmate as she grew. Dad and I played catch with her doll-like body, and she took her first uncertain steps staggering down the hall between us. I fell in love with her peals of laughter, her pluck in regaining her balance and beaming.

We became bound in games to cope with our parents' distress. We played doctor to mock my father's many surgeries— back, heart, hemorrhoids. We operated on each other daily to calm ourselves whenever he was in the hospital and our mother was visiting him. I loved the tickle of the spoons as many plastic checkers masquerading as ruptured discs were removed from my back, stitches taken in my chest with toy wooden drumsticks after my heart bypasses. She loved the pressure when her belly was cut open with a butter knife to remove the red dice portraying her kidney stones. She loved the pats on her buttocks as I sewed them closed with chopsticks.

My mother was losing things in the house, frantic in her searches. We made up a game of guessing what small objects we placed in each other's hands while blindfolded—a thimble, a comb, my mother's lipstick. The tactile sensitivity served us well when we later sought hard-to-find items in drawers and grown-up purses. It later helped us through power blackouts, when we groped to find candles and matches in the dark.

We migrated apart as we made life choices, hers closer to our parents in the Northeast, mine in a distant land in so many ways. My career onstage or on camera was public, while hers was hidden behind the scenes designing elaborate sets for different shows with her boundless artistic talents. Our vernaculars and contexts evolved in vastly different ways as we grew older. Her marriage to her fortress of a second husband, her protector and rescuer, divided us further, shifting her point of view of herself to distressed damsel, helpless, victimized—by me and my parents in a life she had seemed to choose—and always rescued by him. As our parents aged, she made her caretaking look like a fun choice, just like playing doctor had been, and she was adept, efficient, good humored, and diplomatic at it.

Whatever I had said, however innocent my intention, it had been interpreted through filters I did not comprehend. Explaining myself through my own paradigms would not work; she did not like talk of psychology or the vocabulary of emotions. I reviewed incessantly, finding no answer.

I picked up the phone, then dropped it, as she would not be in there even if her "Hello?" was. My underarms ached that I could not hug her to my heart that day, so I lifted my refurbished doll. Then I put her down on my bed as, she was far too hard a doll to hold.

And mourning the sweet sisterhood of our youth, salvaged from the Grand Guignol of our parents' marriage, I held myself instead.

THE UNDERTOW OF NEPTUNE

"**S**o, if you just put your Joan Hancock here and date it there, we're all set," Mr. Neptune said, with a touch of impatience and next to no gravitas. He offered a Neptune Society Pre-need Pen out of the pocket protector of his short-sleeved business shirt, holding it flat in his palm like a weapon. "Any other questions?"

"Yeah, where's the robe and the scythe and the skull and crossbones?" I didn't say.

I took a deep breath, and smoke from the frankincense and candles I'd lit to infuse spirituality into the signing of my cremation contract made me cough. This contract outlined the terms by which I'd be reduced to ashes after death and interred in a big plastic baggie in a wooden box. For the rep, this was a routine he performed several times a day, five days a week. For me, this commitment was momentous.

Yes, I had questions. Most I had struggled to answer on my own in advance. Like, why am I making this decision now?

Simple. I'd recently ended a long relationship and decided to go it alone in life. I wanted to stop waiting for love to determine my future and my future gravesite. I wanted to firm up at least one plan just with me. At this halfway point, forty-nine years old, odds were weighing in favor of death being a real possibility instead of some remote rumor. Death was definite, reliable, something I could count on that could show up well before love ever did. Especially if I bit the bullet and took my own life. Maudlin self-pity arose. I forced it down. That was a last resort. First, I'd have to definitively, irrevocably fail at:

Plan A: Being a successful working actor, married to a wonderful man with great kids.

Plan B: Being a successful working writer, with many readers and distinguished recognition for my output, married to a wonderful man with great kids.

Plan C: Being a teacher of improvisation married to a wonderful man with kids.

Plan D: Being a happy single, successful, charitable community activist alone forever and happy.

Nah. I couldn't foresee that possibility.

So, if things got intolerably much worse, my idea was:

Plan E: To die from unnatural self-inflicted causes. I would take sedatives to stop my mind's perpetual self-abuse. I'd crawl into a trash bag as I yawned, pull the top with the twist-tie in after me, seal the bag, hop out to the curb, clamber into the can, and nap. No muss, no fuss, easiest on everybody if I just disappeared.

Would our contract be nullified, like life insurance, if my corporeal self took the drugs, took a cab out of town, then rolled myself in a stupor into my trash bag and down into a mountain ravine where I could not be found and hence not be incinerated? And, furthermore, if I had no will, and there were no remains, would there be a refund from Neptune? And who would get it?

C'mon, I thought. *Grow up already and make a will and testament. Leave most things to the causes I love, and what's left to the people I resent, the people who had hurt me, who had not been there for me when I needed them but might need the money.* My charitable behest after suicide might make them feel really guilty, and that gave me great sadistic pleasure that might be felt in my next incarnation.

Why was I choosing cremation? Why not go underground like all my elders had in the Jewish cemetery in New Haven?

First, I was claustrophobic. The very idea of being buried in a coffin made me anxious. I didn't trust that my fears would instantly cease with my pulse. I'd also been firmly opposed to being cast out to sea by Mr. Neptune, as I feared water of any depth closing over my head.

Second, I had now lived more of my life in California than in Connecticut, and had no big affinity for my homeland, my family, or Judaism. Plus, if I got buried, who knew what might happen to that location of me later? There could be floods, landmines, quagmires, or, on the West Coast, quakes and seismic shifts.

I recalled how happy my father was that his burial would be under the cemetery's single grand, spreading oak. He felt this was one of his luckiest breaks ever because it would make it easier for folks to find him when they made pilgrimages to visit. But the oak got root rot and died a year after he did, and without the landmark, he was lost to us. Besides, I didn't need to go back to his gravesite to argue with him. I could conjure and fight with him in my own head anytime, anywhere.

Third, ashes were a portable tangible. A reminder of me. Something for folks to be sentimental about, an altar for their mourning me in their very own homes, until they buried me in the sadder deaths of more recent others.

Fourth, I preferred to be packaged in an ecologically correct, functional vessel and for my remains to have a posthumous purpose. I'd asked if Neptune's staff could divide my ashes into small decorative bottles. Or bake me into paperweights or door-stops—maybe with my picture on them. But Mr. Neptune had firmly reminded me that the early-bird, no-frills discount to which I was entitled for signing before the age of fifty would not cover this. And he suggested with some distaste that my afterlife, or after-death, might best be handled by my closest loved ones.

At this moment, I hadn't any. My sister's proximity to our parents and her in-laws on the East Coast had already burdened her with caring for her husband's late grandmother, late mother, and late father in that order, then there was the failing health and demise of our father and the maintenance of our needy moth-er. Although I, long ago relocated to the West Coast, had helped and was still helping to finance some of these deteriorations, I assumed she might find my additional leftovers distasteful.

I had no other significant others into whose care the bone meal of me could be placed, and could word no will and testa-ment, as I had no beloved heirs or intimates at that moment. Until I could create a document with no snide recriminations, I'd hold off on making a will.

Mr. Neptune's luxurious eyebrows were assembling in the shape of a question mark. I felt rushed.

I still wanted to ask how the crematorium functioned, and if it resembled Auschwitz in any way. But this ample man, in his short-sleeved button-down tucked unattractively into wool trou-sers in mid-July, was not Jewish. He might not comprehend my inherited horror.

Did I have any more questions about my demise that he could answer? That anyone could answer?

Mainly, would my ashes be as lonely as I was—or are ashes

oblivious? I had a starvation for love that seemed eternal, that even death would not deter. He was wearing a wedding band— he probably would not understand my midlife, never-married, free-floating-in-outer-space panic. He was not a cleric or a psychiatrist, nor was empathy one of his job requirements. What, I might ask, even qualified him to have such power over my fate? I gave it one last try.

"Sir," I spoke as formally as the wording of the documents in question, as if in a court of law. "Thank you for your patience. What if I were to someday fall in love with someone with whom I wished to be interred in a shared plot or box? If such good fortune befell me, would Neptune give me my money back?"

"I'm afraid not," he said. "Your investment covers the cost of keeping your records, we hope, for a long, long time; of making your arrangements; and of having your wishes carried out as quickly as possible after you pass on."

The chemicals that constitute dread rose up my esophagus with a mulch of urgent questions.

Wait. Did I really want to know all the gory details about my aftermath? I asked myself.

Such as: If I continued my tendency to be this alone, how specifically would Neptune be notified to gather me?

Would there be a special cleaning service that took care of post-demise fumigation? Judging from the increasing odor of me at this moment, things might get much worse later.

Could I sneak a peek ahead at the epilogue? Would anybody hold a memorial service? Who would speak, what would they say, and what music would they play?

I longed to philosophize with this good Christian gentleman about what lay beyond for a lapsed Jewess and devout atheist, but our beliefs could clash. My idea of a heavenly afterlife was that I'd find all the things I had lost in life—those earrings, single socks, a favorite green hat, my leopard umbrella, ex-boyfriends. Their hiding places would all be revealed to me in flashbacks. "Oh, *that's* where that went," I'd exclaim. I was still mad at myself for letting those precious things slip out of my life—a piece of my mind has been actively seeking my old peacoat since the eighties.

I was diving deep into the insignificance of my death and getting rather blue, when Mr. Neptune coughed and wiped his eyes of smoke-induced sting.

"I'm sorry—I have a lunch meeting at some distance. You can mail these in if you need more time to think things through, but let me say this, off the record."

His tone gentler, he looked kindly into my face and spoke from no canned Neptune pre-need notes.

"There's so much you can't know now: when, where, how. I certainly understand your wish to be economical. However, if you were to meet the love of your life, wouldn't it be worth a couple thousand dollars of loss to surrender your contract if need be? Or, better yet, if you refer him to Neptune, this future love could get a discount on a matching basic container, or half of a red oak box to be shared with you."

Did somebody say discount? If my truest love got a discount, I guess it would be just as good as my getting it because I loved him selflessly. That's how love was rumored to operate. My heart lifted in joyous anticipation of sharing this news with my hypothetical love—it would be a form of dowry.

"So, this is reversible?"

"Of course. No one will track you down to cremate you if you deauthorize our contract—you'll just forfeit this fee. We could renegotiate later on, and we will consider that you signed up pre-need."

I was touched. If there was any eternal in my future, I would be eternally grateful for Mr. Neptune's wisdom, mercy, and tolerance that fateful afternoon.

So, I firmly signed and dated the contract, now hoping against hope to lose the goddamned fee by falling in forever love. Then I maybe I'd get a queen-size burial plot or a double-size ash box from Mr. Neptune to share with my beloved sleepmate-to-come. Either way, I'd be covered. And for now, I was appeased. I had so much to look forward to.

CAR-ISMA

I n 2003, I accidentally dated an alcoholic. He came as an accessory on my Prius.

I got to know the handsome Johnny O. (not his whole name) while I awaited the delivery of the hybrid he promised would arrive in four days. And during the four weeks I was dropping in on the dealership to check on my hotly anticipated car, he began courting me in a car-man kind of way, demonstrating how his smart key could open my vehicle without even touching it, teaching me how to change its oil, change a tire, hotwire a car—skills I'd never use, but I sure liked the way he was teaching me. He'd worry, he said, if I were abandoned along a roadside somewhere: fearful, cheerless, and Johnny O.-less. This flirt rolled the odometer back on my feminism thirty years. Asexual for months, I got suddenly hormonal, helpless, horny, and girly.

He'd recently moved to Los Angeles from a small town. Promoted to manager of a big-city dealership of the car du jour, he was at the very top of his game. He wanted to celebrate—anything and everything.

"You did a radio commercial for Lipitor? Baby, let's party."

We had little in common. I was Jewish, he was Catholic. He knew nothing about acting, except what he read in *People*. I knew nothing of engines, except what he highlighted for me in *Road &*

Track. Talking to him was like traveling to exotic lands without shots, bags, or passports.

He was saving me so much on future gas, I owed it to him to go dancing with him, he said. Besides, as a lapsed celebrity, then best known as the voice of a cable cartoon character, I'd legitimize him in the show biz world. When Johnny O. spun me some salsa moves in the showroom, dipping me breathless in his pumped-up arms to gaze into his bottomless eyes, I wanted him to close the deal, wanted him under my hood, wanted his dipstick in my oil. For an artist in search of a subject, I rationalized, dating him would be research.

I wore really old underwear and brought three gal pals along to the club to slow things down. After watching his groovy moves to music, they were no help.

"I'd fuck him for a Prius," said one.

"I'd fuck him for a Civic," said another.

"Any floor models left like him?" asked the third.

I became a pimp for Johnny O. types, fully loaded, ethnic, dancing pretty boys who offered clean machines, fast delivery, and free floor mats to my friends.

"Baby, you are so good for my business," said Johnny. "Let me be good for you. Let me Scotchgard your seats, give you rear air bags, put a nice finish on your body."

And so he did.

California was car country, and my Prius dealer became my personal pinup boy. For me, my shiny new hunchback hybrid and my shiny new guy were ecological, liberated statements. For him, ours was a marriage made in some nutty narcissistic heaven of social climbing. He loved greeting my famous neighbors on the streets each morning. He timed his smokes to catch their dog-walking, giving my conversation piece of a car a rubdown, showing off his conversation piece of a butt every day at 7:00 a.m. He sold two on my block.

He was spending more and more time at my house, in my bed, in my head, and moving down the drive train to my heart.

Silly me, I never did learn how to have sex out of gear, without engaging "the clutch." Infatuated, lapsed Jewess, child of teetotalers that I was, I thought he was just a social drinker, like the Brits or the French. I didn't recognize the signs, like his magnetic personality that could pull women out of the plumbing—he'd go to the men's room and come back with groupies. His Marlboro Man appeal to guys—he could shape himself to the needs of any lookie-loo on the lot with such sincerity. He could sell people car packages they never knew they wanted: leather seats to animal rights activists, hybrids to Hummer lovers, navigational systems to agoraphobics. He had *car-isma*.

Yet as a visitor to my world, he was raw and awkward. I had a Pygmalion complex, and he became my perfect pig, enjoying some ballets by my side, sipping from his silver flask.

"Nice rack on the fairy princess, eh? Whoa, get a load of the package on that swan boy."

Such a fresh perspective.

He celebrated his first Hanukkah with me with great respect, rocking a yarmulke at Temple Isaiah. He was made very welcome and handed out his card promiscuously.

Then on Christmas Eve he told me he was going caroling with his dealers—I thought he meant *car*. He staggered into my bed at dawn with an unnatural snow falling from his nose hairs, smelling like the puke he'd parked on my front stoop. He slept seventeen hours, looking delicious even drooling. I woke him

Christmas night to tell him I felt scared—scared of the addiction thing, scared of the improvisational vomiting thing, scared we wouldn't work out.

"But, baby, I can't make it here without you!"

He begged my forgiveness. He pledged on bended knee that he'd give up booze and cigarettes for me *forever*.

Oh, how I wanted to believe him. He was so beautiful—with his hearty laugh, his golden skin, his adoring eyes. I mistook his hungry kisses for commitments, his bended knee as a practice posture for a sexy married life. I mistook his need for me for love of me. I gave him another chance and dove deeper.

Two drinkless weeks later, he developed tics and twitches, animated an entire new personality out of them—a frenetic, unglued, uncool new self. Sobriety was hurting his sales and social networking. And when he squashed an addiction down in one place, it would just pop out in another. He developed an oral fixation, reeking of breath mints and chewing tobacco. His shaky hand spilled his constant cup of coffee. His gum-chewing, toothpick-bearing, overactive mouth made him seem low-class. He had flop sweat. He was anxious, putting on weight. He overslept and got docked commissions. He struggled to be what I wanted him to be.

But I learned that for him, *forever* meant until he forgot, and that *sober* just meant no alcohol. I became enmeshed in a fantasy of fixing him. For me, an unemployed actress starved for purpose, the role of appetite suppressant, pacifier, nag, and room deodorizer was the only identity I had.

Then, I caught him smoking crack with his friendly local prostitute and freaked. He followed me out to my Prius, which I'd hazard parked behind my usual guest spot at his place, which was now filled by another woman's shiny red Ford.

"This won't work," I seethed.

"Right, baby. You're too good for me," he whined.

"What?! No, no, I'm not. I'm not!" I cried, fighting for the man's *soul*, but really for my now desperate attachment, while my unambiguous inner voice was bellowing, *Get the hell out!*

But he leaped off the wagon and went on a career-ending bender, and I agonized. Even though I'd banned him from my bed until he cleaned up his act, my mind was drowning in my fantasy dreamboat's undertow. I crammed the CliffNotes on addiction into my head. I surfed the Internet all night long, trying to understand the mental quagmire the twelve steps stepped one out of. I couldn't let go. I started researching a meeting I could drive Johnny O. to, hoping I could heal him and by healing him maybe heal me.

I was astounded. There were many different meetings for substance abusers of all kinds happening every hour everywhere in Los Angeles. Those hordes of people chain-smoking and chugging coffee outside churches were attending all kinds of programs: for food, drink, drug, and gambling addicts, for people who loved the addicts, for the children and parents of the addicts, for the fetuses of the addicts. And I was now a psycho hypochondriac, identifying with every single one.

I had never realized there existed all these islands of choice and all this vocabulary for being damaged. Identifying myself according to this paradigm, I now had so much more in common with Johnny O. I was a longtime acting addict, addicted to unmarriageable men. I was a recovering thumb-sucker, now forty years sober. Now I was an addict hooked on an addict who was hooked on a hooker who was hooking him on crystal meth. Why, we could go to meetings together.

She found my number in his cell phone and called her fellow Johnny O.-aholic to gloat late one night.

"Honey, I know Johnny O. liked you a lot, but he's marrying me this summer," she slurred. "And he's getting me a Prius that gets over fifty-two miles per gallon in city driving."

"Hah," I retorted as I hung up the phone and my hung-up heart. I knew she'd never get that kind of mileage. I now knew every girl gets to get over a bad boy named Johnny once in her life. This was my turn.

AT HER WEDDING I KNEW

Melancholy grayed the day as he propelled me along a stone path toward a forest cathedral. Sunbeams filtered down through the high boughs of the redwoods, highlighting his few remaining hairs.

I hated how cruelly I was now judging him and myself—this after spending sequential weekends together in intimate conversations and positions, agreeing to go off for this, our first weekend away, the promise of consummation unspoken. Facing the last dregs of our fifties, we were infused with intensified chemistry. We were desperate. We knew we might be each other's last chance.

We seemed so appropriate. He was a freelance Jewish person like me, with a distinguished position in city government and a great golden retriever. I earned my own living, owned my own home, cooked well, made a nice appearance. We shared cultural references and dance moves. We were different enough in ways that had felt complementary since we'd met—until just last night at a dinner, when I overheard him say a couple surprising things.

"I won't be voting for Obama." Then later, "When I get married, I'll want to keep kosher."

Shock shot through my body twice. With this sudden reveal of his drift from Undecided to Republican, from a Reformed to a more Conservative Jew, and now his style of steering me along like I had no capacity to walk on my own, the possibility of an "us" was quickly deconstructing in my mind. We would be far too out of step in the larger world.

The painful realization that I could no longer choose this once very desirable man couldn't have occurred at a more ironic time, with the swell of a cello quartet rising toward a too-blue sky, guiding us to his cousin's wedding ceremony. A searing pain began shoving my eyeballs into my skull, making my eyes water and my nose sniffle.

He handed me his hanky with suspicion. Phlegming his monogram, I recalled how I adored his gallantry when we began: the opening of the car door, the bestowing of his jacket on chilly nights, the walking on the outside, the picking up of the check. But my daffy fantasies of a future with an old-fashioned, protective, take-charge guy were disintegrating.

I refolded the handkerchief to hide my evidence.

"I'll get this cleaned," I said.

Another item of his I'd have to return, along with the slippers, shaver, and toothbrush he'd left at my home in month three of sweet weekends there.

"What's going on?" he asked.

"I always cry at weddings," I said.

"You started in the parking lot."

"I like to start early, avoid the crush."

I'd just met his extended family the evening before at the rehearsal supper. I'd enjoyed their cultured conversations, their family jokes, our lefty liberal laughter, far more than I had his sudden righteous-winged rant about Democrats late last night. Damn. His kin could have been my family, except that my doorway into them—him—was closing. Never again date an Undecided, I swore.

No more control freaks, I pledged. Never again meet a man's family in the first trimester of a relationship, I vowed.

Now, there they all were, assembled on redwood plank risers around a flower-festooned dais. Many waved warmly. Several competed to clear space for us, the couple-in-training, to sit near them. *Being near new couples is reassuring for longtime married couples,* I thought as I clambered their way. *It validates their lifestyle. It vulgarizes the freedoms, vagaries, varieties, and unknowns of the sinful single life. Longtime couples welcome panicky new girlfriends like me, seducing them desperately into the stultifying sameness of a million anniversaries spent kissing the same man's mouth.*

Who was I kidding? Such familiarity would be wonderful if I were in love. But I now knew, keenly and inconveniently, that this was not "the one." He had been somebody's one, as he'd been long married, and was now divorced with a daughter I'd met and liked. He had relationship cred. Mine was nil. I'd never found nor been a permanent "one." I had always been the odd woman out. At fifty-nine, I felt as though I had a scarlet letter *N* on my chest for *Never.* I was the perpetual Ms. mismatch.

He aimed me and my strenuous grin toward his older cousin, Laura. She embraced me to her maternal bosom. I surrendered with shame at receiving comfort under false pretenses. Maybe she imagined I was whimpering tears of joy for my own unscheduled nuptials with her virile cousin, my heart softening with surrender to his masculinity.

He is a jerk, I'd realized at the hotel check-in yesterday, after a testy discussion of why I should put the bill on my Visa.

"Because you can write this trip off for business," he pontificated.

"How do you figure that?" I challenged.

"Because you might teach a workshop here!" he snapped.

"That's *completely* hypothetical," I groused.

Our sneering upper lips, drying like beached fish on our bared front teeth, repositioned themselves into smiles for the benefit of the hotelier. If she looked closely—but she didn't, as a huge crowd was clogging the lobby awaiting rooms—she might have noticed that manic look in the eyes of a couple whose minds fear they've made a mistake before their muscles can take action to rectify it. She might have seen the spasms in the corners of the manufactured smiles that came not from happy anticipation of the king-size bed, Jacuzzi, and bay view to come, but from acting as if all was well—the most aberrant thing two people whose affections are mutating can do to one another.

The soon-to-be weds glided from different ends of the forest toward the platform where the merger would occur, and the musicians struck up "Here Comes the Bride." My date's middle-aged cousin approached her far younger, online miracle man with confidence and radiance. I must have looked like a madwoman, with teardrops dragging flakes of supposedly waterproof mascara down my face into his decimated handkerchief. I never did learn how to cry pretty.

The fiancées reached the rabbi and faced each other with delight tinged with sensuous secrets and eternal gazes. I could have just puked as a collective "Aww" exuded from the group. Most of his family members had been married forever, betrothed prenatally, it seemed, and still seemed to like each other. The contrast between their endurance and the spasms in my neck from being forced onto my pre-ex's shoulder for comfort or maybe concealment was vast.

"Do you take this man to be your husband, through sickness and health, for richer or . . ."

And his cousin, as if afraid her Jdate darling might disappear, shouted, "I *do*!"

■

"You most certainly do NOT!" he'd yelled earlier that evening, slamming our room door, his proboscis reddening. This wasn't the nose I'd found so adorable when he'd first aimed it to kiss me. This snout had now been repurposed for snorting. "You have no right to leave tonight!"

"I'll pay you back for my ticket," I said. "And I'll pay any penalties and half the hotel bill you paid, too. Staying together now feels wrong. I'm so sorry."

"How cruel you are."

Had the poor man known how my dislike was distorting my perceptions, he'd have realized I was actually being kind. I recoiled as his cologne putrefied his musk, his hairy hands grew apelike, and his face and expansive scalp revealed a map of dermatological misfortunes.

I stayed for a festive evening, both of us forcing laughter over lumps in our throats, avoiding his family's future invitations; Tefloning our pressed-together bodies from true contact. I wept on his shoulder as we waltzed, partly from sadness at losing this once dear friend and his fabulous dog from my life, but mostly because I ached to be resting in the arms of the right man.

The shoulder of his expensive suit dampening, he hissed, "Now what?!"

"I'm sorry, so sorry."

I slipped away after the dance into the night alone. I was sad for us both as our scaffold of trust toppled, knowing we'd both be starting all over again from zero. But I was glad to miss the newlyweds mainlining love full-throttle into each other's eyes. I yearned for my loving gaze to be fully met at my own wedding.

AN OFFERING

I'm acting less, writing more and liking it, now that I can reflect on the past with a less bitter aftertaste, now that I can imagine a future alone without acid thoughts scorching my brain from the inside out, now that I've been found innocent of my own accusations, now I'm no longer filled with thoughts of inferiority needing immediate vindication, and can frequently gaze at myself and the world with warmth. I finally have a voice talking the desperate one down from the edge.

Now that I'm sixty-three, I learn about myself from what I write, not from how others react. Instead of peering through the headache of seeing how I'm being seen, I *see*. Words do the heavy lifting my performing body used to do. I'm learning to say far more in fewer words and sometimes in none.

This warm, supportive teacher provides us prompts—triggers to inspire our stream-of-consciousness, to shake us out of habits, to egg us on to explore. Her prompt, "What can you not help noticing?" is a rich starting point. Despite the lovely Malibu surroundings, the hibiscus in full bloom, the ocean and sky demanding our eyes drift out to their shared edge, my subject is blatantly obvious.

Wendy's women's writing workshop is the perfect place for a single heterosexual female to park a solo life.

I can't help noticing the many here—smart, talented, each writing in a singular voice. Full of love with much to offer. Some older, some younger; some have done it all, some not yet, some have lost a lot of it. Some feel ill-equipped for the coming world and pray to earn and learn their way. Some feel they're too raw, some too seasoned, and some too self-sufficient for any companion to complement. I've felt all of it.

Each sends up flares for love—a special color or a signature scent for herself and others to appreciate. Each plays up a favorite part of her body with accoutrements that accessorize, accentuate, and exaggerate what she knows makes her special—her décolletage framed in silk, eyes with kohl, hands with works of bejeweled art, or hair and face au naturel. Each has indelible character, beauty like no other on earth. We all receive compliments, behaving as though we're unaware of the effect they have. We all flaunt our best aspects with nonchalance as we grow more confident week by week. But even naked, shorn of our skin-deep style assertions, the essential us would still shine singular—I can hear it in the originality of our writings.

Your poems hint at unharvested eroticism, your voices tease of love songs still to sing, pleasures yet to know. Your essays tell of injuries survived, strengths gleaned from wounds. You tell stories of love, its promise, and its loss from so many perspectives and, like a psycho-hypochondriac, I feel I've experienced all of them in some role I was playing in work or life.

But I no longer think of myself as fragmented. I think I contain multitudes in a wide range. Just like I've been as an actor, as a writer I can feel and write life from myriad points of view. I'm a character actor and now a character writer, as well. I enjoy the dialogue I imagine emitting from the many characters, male and female, in my play, my screenplay, my musical, in my fantasy of a real life love scene that has a happy ending.

In a matter of weeks, I've fallen in love with the ways each of these women express, applaud each tale they tell. I hear their unique calls to be heard and loved back, much like I heard my mother's when I was a child. Hers repulsed me—I was too little to give her all she needed so badly. But I am bigger now and love and admire many women and have grown particularly fond of you.

If I were a man, I'd appreciate and embrace all you offer, mine the mysteries that could heal us both when solved. We could become the keys that fit each other's locks to inner worlds, the bodies that shape to our backs, the psyches that mesh with our minds. I feel you. I wish I could fill you. I wish I could be man enough to love you all.

If polygamy were legal, I'd propose right now. I'd wed you sequentially, then bed you together in an orgy of mutual appreciation so you could treasure and pleasure in each other, too—such a wondrous natural resource you all are. There'd be plenty to go around instead of not enough. I'd savor all your special recipes, sensitize myself to your traumas, buy you your favorite lotions, massage your hurt places. I'd call, I'd bring flowers, scratch each itch, lick them, stick it to you in the style I'd learn you like, carry you across your thresholds to pleasure. I'd embrace your problem parents, your kids misshapen by an overwhelmed mother with no good man to help out. I see you so easily, as I am you.

Unless and until a worthy one comes along, I will implore you to please carry me as your inner adorer. I'll be the one who sees you, approves you, who holds the treasure of you in my heart, who stokes your radiance from within, the mother or father or lover or god you always needed.

I finally have the courage to love without inhibition. I feel big enough to understand and care for you, but I wasn't always. I was misshapen. I was a child with needs in neon, who grew porcupine quills. I was lonely to the point of despair. I mistook pity and need for love. I thought no one had ever been as bottom-of-the-sea alone as me. I sought a life's companion. I made a million mistakes— loved too soon, stayed too long, left too soon, loved too late. I calculated, strategized, underachieved, aborted, failed over and over again. I found all fault in my unlovability, my undependability and I lost faith, lost confidence, lost interest in life. I ached through many decades. I expressed my excess love through my talent, regardless of whether it was loved back, because it insisted on coming through me no matter what. It's always been my most dependable companion, my battle cry of hope.

All your feelings were mine, too. And if I could have felt for myself all the compassion and admiration you evoke from me today, I might've found contentment with myself far faster.

Please receive my recognition and let it make a difference to you. Because for the longest period of my life, I've been—and I will always be—you.

And for all of us, as long as we're alive and celebrating ourselves, not willing to sell ourselves out, there is always hope for us to be fully met, to fully love and be loved.

LE CRI DU COEUR

Despite being a devout feminist in my mid-sixties, in my heart I remained a boy-crazy, girlish romantic. I wanted equal rights, choice, and a voice to match a man's in power, yet I fantasized about being swept up in a helpless love. My free spirit flew untethered but longed to share an earthbound life. I wanted to cook for the guy who'd open the jars, primp for the guy who'd take out the trash, tidy up after a beloved who tidied me in other ways. I was so ashamed of how much I wanted to get married that I acted way blasé about it.

"Hey. If it happens, it happens."

It wasn't happening.

The old-fashioned good fortune of encountering appropriate men in the flesh eluded me, as I rarely left my house. They hadn't found me in bars or bookstores, because I never went. No one fixed me up, as I was hard to fit. So, I would send my love-call into cyberspace despite having had disappointing experiences on three different dating sites.

1. An intense animal attraction with a cat lover was aborted by his comforting his feral cat's feelings over mine as it nipped and scratched at me.

2. A third date with a person with a great pedigree soured

when he backed hard into a parked car, then asked me, "Do you think I should just take off?"

3. After an auspicious month of meals out, a man divulged he was in kidney failure and on a long waitlist for a donation. Clutching my kidneys, I donated my deepest regrets.

But life looked shorter these days. And having graduated at last from therapy with a degree in listening to my body instead of my rationales, I would go once more into the breach. Building up a reserve of courage and specific questions, I decided to seek a new crop through the Match.com portal. This time, instead of wasting disappointing days answering only the online guys who picked me first, I would widen my parameters and make the first move toward men I found desirable.

After weeks of sorting through men with good driver discounts, healthy kidneys, and no cats, I harvested two shiny new finds. I had just written friendly words to the impressive global guitarist, A., when the thoughtful writing and thumbnail photo of psychologist S. captivated me, as evidenced by perspiration forming on my upper lip and underarms. I composed two wholesome well-worded lines of interest to S., not wanting to give the impression I was easy because I wrote first. Within ten minutes, he'd responded in five lines with two exclamation points saying how much he enjoyed reading my profile. My face flushed, and my silly heart thumped like I was twelve. We had a quick volley of messages; we would meet a few days later. Meantime, A. wrote and asked me to tea the next day. I said yes—he seemed like a good guy, and I strategized that I needed an immediate backup plan to avoid the putting-too-many-eggs-in-one-basket-out-of-scarcity trip.

I had A. meet me at a golf course coffee shop where we could always watch the golfers if chat dried up. Fortunately, A. and I had many art and musical contexts in common. We soon began the discreet but accelerated tactic of divulging histories of past relationships. Neither of us had ever been married. He'd recently separated from his longtime girlfriend, let's call her X., now his best friend forever. I confessed that I wanted very much to be married in the next round and didn't want to attract any misfires along the way.

He asked me to go hear music sometime. I told him I was heading to NYC for a couple weeks—true, but a delaying tactic, so I could think about him from a distance a bit as my body was having zero reactions—and would call when I got back. A. offered that his BFF, his ex X., had a New York apartment she rented out by the week—would I be interested?

"Sure!" I said.

Later that day, my first phone chat with the psychologist, S., got us eager to speak in person. I was mystified, as his erudite voice sounded so different than his cute little picture looked. He was new to Los Angeles and asked to take me to appetizers at a place I chose. I sent him websites of three, $, $$, and $$$. He chose $$$. *Promising,* I thought. *He's already making an investment.*

We met on a Monday for happy hour at the bar of a pricey hotel, embraced like friends, and, entranced, soon moved on to their fine dining. Our four-hour conversation escalated in openness, predicting good emotional chemistry, so much so that he felt compelled to tell me he'd been seeing someone for a month, but, he said, "I know she's not the one."

I thanked him for telling me and told myself to proceed with caution. He said he'd like to see me again before I left for New York. I said yes. Then, he patted his pants, ransacked his jacket pockets, sputtering, apologizing—he had forgotten his wallet.

"That's what they all say," I said, my heart sinking, the moistening, erectile parts of my body dehydrating and retracting. *Please don't let this cute guy be a con man.*

I slapped down a credit card, but he insisted on being the boy and treating, saying he'd send a check if I'd give my address. When I hesitated, he asked if we instead could get together a few days later to attend an event at a large local theater to end violence toward women. If I met him there, he would pay me in person.

How manipulative a man might this be, inviting me to an Eve Ensler event on a second date, I thought. But he was so apologetic, and my desire for him to keep his word and give me my money back so strong, I agreed.

When we met for the show, he handed me a check. We had an even better time, and he asked me out for the following Monday night. First, I cashed the check, and it cleared. My body sighed in relief. Then I let my fantasies fly. He was intelligent, if forgetful, he was a father of two prefab perfect-looking kids, and he was funny and adorable. I didn't want to put my heart at risk if this wasn't real. I didn't want to be his "weeknight woman" while he *shtupped* someone else.

We met for supper, and I told him that if he had a two-day, sleepover weekend romantic partner, I didn't want to be his back-up girl. He said he and the woman weren't romantic, just sexual, and he was sure neither of them would care much when it ended. I doubted that, as I know the skewed lens through which men view their affairs. It differed radically from most women's. Plus, he had no idea what a treasure he was by LA standards. But after being burned so much, I was resolute about maintaining my inner peace and said I wouldn't communicate further while he was seeing this other woman.

He said, "I'll end it."

With caution I said, "Please don't do that for me, as we have no idea what we are, but I don't think I can see you again, if you're not honest with both of us and yourself."

"Okay," he replied soberly.

So away I flew to the East Coast, scared about losing, but proud of myself for taking a stand for what I wanted, not settling for sloppy seconds, and not betraying a woman I'd never met.

A few days later, the guitarist, A., emailed me that his ex X's NY apartment wasn't available after all, but that he was looking forward to seeing me when I got back. I got zero body response besides friendliness. He then asked if, by the way, I was seeing a man named S. *Huh?* I thought.

Yes, I wrote. *But how could you know that?*

Because I told my ex, X., I was going out with you, and she just called me crying that S. broke up with her to go out with you.

But why would she think that? I emailed, hitting the keys too hard, misspelling everything.

Because she broke up with me to go out with him. I told her that I'd met and liked you, and I showed off your profile online, and she saw he had friended you on Facebook the same exact day as I did, and she guessed.

I'm shell-shocked, have shooting pains under my arms. What are the odds? Just then, I see a FB message from this woman, X. warning me that S. is a two-timer, that he led her on, that they've been lovers for many weeks, that she had been sure he was her "one."

This is way TMI for me. *How small and incestuous a world have I fallen into,* I'm thinking. *I've seen this guy three times, and*

I'm already being cyber-stalked, caught in the middle of a creepy love quadrangle. My scalp and skin were crawling, my teeth gnashing, stomach queasing. I took a breath and answered X. that I've been in her shoes and it hurts, and that sometimes a person who rejects us seems far more important than they should be, and that I hope she finds the right man for her, acknowledging that he might not be the one for me, either. I thanked her for her warning, which I thought was way out of line, yet made me mistrustful of S. I had no idea where the truth lay, but I valued my peace too much to get involved with a player.

Sad and resolved, I go to look at his profile one last time before I let the wishful glimmer of an "us" go, but it has been removed.

"Maybe he has found the one," the site teases. "Maybe you will, too!"

He emailed and asked to fetch me from the airport on the Saturday night I returned. Despite my concerns my mind got excited. Then, even as the flight's arrival was delayed from eight till nine till midnight till 2:00 a.m., he waited for me. He hugged me in a friendly way when I arrived and took me to an all-night diner for a serious talk over steak and eggs. He picked up the check.

And the conversation would continue.

HE'S BEEN US

*T*his women's writing workshop has been our womb, our incubator of ideas and new friendships for two years. I'm grateful for this group. You've been my audience, my critics and advisers. I'm writing nearly full-time now and take myself more seriously since I've had pieces published and have performed things I developed here in your company. I've thrilled at your growth into fine artists and absorbed all your stories as you've honed your breathtaking work.

Whereas my writing was once a hobby, filler to kill time between acting jobs, I now consider acting jobs small stalls in my writing. I take my laptop everywhere, like a lover I can lug in my backpack.

But now I have a flesh lover with strong shoulders to carry it. I'm thinking they will one day carry his things and move them into my house. I can even imagine us marrying if he asks me. I tell you this, sirens, because I want to ignite your hope. It's not my intent to gloat. If it lifts your heart to hear, read on. If it hurts, or resonates with lack, just skip the next page.

Against all odds, I've found a cohort who will fill in big blanks on my pages—who moistens dry spots in my pen, head, heart, and other regions. Beside him, I'm not beside myself with nerves, and he calms, too. I face the injustices of this world with more faith to fight them. I feel joy and hope. If a paradoxical person like him could happen to a *complicated person like me, it can happen to you, if you want it to.*

He is an intellectual hunk, an academic who lisps. He's pro-found yet silly. He gestures wildly when he speaks, even on his cell phone—if only he could harness that energy to power its bat-tery. When he laughs, most often at himself, at a joke he's about to tell just before the punchline, he doubles over, hands to knees as though weeping and heaving. He is devoted to inner peace, but craves documentaries about Hitler and the Holocaust at bedtime. And amid these idiosyncrasies lurks a beautiful soul. I have never loved anyone normal, and he's just abnormal enough to love my many quirks back. Paired in orbit, our oddness is turning to even-ness. Our jagged jigsaw puzzle-pieces rounded by deep talk, we are fitting into a colorful finished picture that makes beautiful sense.

He's a psychologist, a tuning fork for others' feelings. He puts himself in others' shoes, resonates with the labyrinths of meaning behind their words. Me, too, as an actor/writer. We speak subtext, share the languages of suffering and humor in our shop talk. Like me, he admits to mistakes. He hasn't the guile or the desire to lie, is aroused far more by the risks of telling the truth.

I can't say our courtship has been smooth sailing, as we both sift-ed through scar tissue, sorted through twisted prisms of perception, removed our projections from our observations. But tidal waves re-ceded to swells, roadblocks smoothed to speed bumps, black marks faded to smudges, and scarlet flags paled to pink, as we recognized our hurts in each other. See, he's spent the longest period of his life like us, too—a leftover solo act who couldn't find the right fit in love.

In writings to come in our final few weeks, I'll invite you to peer through the peephole to see how I survive and, I hope, thrive in this courtship-in-progress. I will share the lore in various—originally deplorable, yet in retrospect adorable—versions of our origin story.

DEADLY BEDDING

It was nightmarish enough sleeping alone for a sensitive person like me. I'd wake up to find my face scarred from mashing into my pillow, my knee dislocated, my ear bent over and aching, and freak out. Sometimes this princess and her pee would awaken in the wee hours of the night to stagger to the bathroom on feet that had become painful stumps.

"Wait—can these be my feet?" I'd ask the unsympathetic air. "Did someone switch them in the night?"

Living so long on my own, I slept lightly, keeping my ears open to nighttime sounds in the big cities I preferred. Discerning the noises of a neighbor being normal from a beheading in progress was a survival skill. For security, I'd have one eye open keeping watch while the other eye did its REMs, then switch. I'd awake walleyed, but grateful to be alive for another day.

When my allergist told me I was breathing in dust mites from my feathered bedding, that was the last straw—and the last down I ever enjoyed. I got even more fanatical, throwing toxic pillows into the dryer on the highest heat each week to kill all the creatures and suck out their corpses.

To preserve a seamless sleep, I began to measure how many ounces of water I could drink for how many hours of rest. Four ounces, I'd wake up at 2:00 a.m.; two ounces, I could maybe make it till 5:00 a.m. But if I drank no water at all, I'd wake up swollen-tongued, like dead cattle during the Dust Bowl. Sippy cups, Tempur-Pedic pillows, mattress protectors, lavender eye masks, knee dividers—there were worlds of merchandise taking away the money I hid under my hypoallergenic latex mattress, and taking away the intimacy I so desired.

Then through the miracle of cyberspace came the love call of handsome S. He was very understanding of my sensitivities, as he had so many of his own. We began meeting for long suppers, then risked the contamination of love or other insidious infections by holding hands on long walks, talking, and talking. Soon our waking hours weren't enough to contain our enthusiasm for each other. It was time to take that next big step—and sleep together. But not to have sex—oh, no. We weren't ready for that. Just to *sleep* together. We negotiated this exhaustively and got to first base by accident one day, collapsing into an afternoon nap. Waking up to find him there smiling at me felt so right.

"I'm shy," I said, "about moving too fast."

"Me, too, but our being together feels inevitable."

"It does, I agree." I was thrilled. "I sleep in baggy cotton stuff."

"So do I," he exclaimed.

"I'm a pillow-holic," I giggled.

"Me, too," he cried. "I have six."

"I like 'em soft," I whispered.

"I like 'em hard," he implied.

"I'm a morning person."

"I'm . . . a night guy."

"I'm a light sleeper."

"I snore," he confessed.

"I have earplugs," I offered.

"I . . . have a sleep apnea machine."

"No!" we cried. How could such easy daytime companionship coexist with such nighttime incompatibility? We had too much going for us. We had to try. Spending the night together would be our Everest.

We embarked on the climb equipped with the coziest of T-shirts and shorts with 2,000-thread count pillow covers and sheets and crept onto his wall-to-wall, extra-firm California king.

We were far too thrilled to sleep those first nights, with lots of adjusting to do in the cuddle phase. Living alone so long, I hadn't realized how bony I'd become. My ribs were unable to tolerate his arm, and my neck was incapable of resting on his shoulder for more than a minute. My arm on his chest inhibited his rest, my leg over his made him claustrophobic.

We put pillows in the problem spots, and patience in the learning curve.

The third night, delirious from lack of sleep, I earplugged and blindfolded myself into sensory deprivation as he read in the prison floodlight sweeping his half of the acreage. With him keeping watch, I could finally doze, keeping both eyes closed. What a relief—until he turned off the light. Then his noisy breathing degenerated into multisyllabic snores, punctuated by desperate snorts of near suffocation that penetrated my earplugs and my heart. Far from irked, I felt like I had to keep a vigil so he wouldn't die on me.

At 4:00 a.m. I discovered that if I made regular little kissing sounds, I could interrupt his snores and get intermittent snatches of sleep with pillows around my ears.

The next morning, we awoke to debrief.

"Boy, do you snore!" I said.

"Yeah? Well, you make these weird little sucking noises all night."

One week in, I'd synchronized my sleep with his quiet, waking every few minutes with his noise. Twenty winks would have to suffice. I'd catnap during the day.

As a psychologist, his empathy for my sleeplessness was keen. Tenderhearted, he felt empathic, became afraid to disturb or kill me with his restless leg syndrome karate kicks and elbow chops. He'd creep away to another room to leave me in peace, but I'd miss him and crawl out of bed to kiss him. Like in O. Henry's *Gift of the Magi*, we each sacrificed our precious rest for our growing affection.

Infatuation drowned out need for rest as lust came creeping and sex came leaping and came and came again. Living together would be the next logical step. But first we committed to trying it out, and he'd stay over most nights with an occasional foray back to his bachelor flat so we could both evaluate. We were missing each other, getting more and more embedded.

Like new parents giving birth to our baby love, nursing its newness in our shared crib, we knew we might never sleep through the night again. But with no risk of pregnancy and no critics of our middle-aged good fortune, sleep was our little dragon to slay, our romantic gauntlet to run.

At first, it got more difficult as he got more comfortable in my house. The sweetest man by day, by night S. was a sociopath. Gentle Dr. Jekyll would hide a nocturnal Mr. Hyde until, drowsing into bed at two, he'd head-butt me unconscious in his try for a goodnight kiss, clap my eardrums to bursting in his attempt to clasp my face to his, or kiss my eyeball, widened in panic, before it could flinch. Asleep, this well-mannered man had no etiquette.

Sometimes he'd pull my pillow out from under my head, leaving it to thud onto my extra-firm mattress. He'd roll away from me with the covers, exposing me to frostbite, then roll onto me, pinning me. I'd just lie like a mummy, gazing at him by the glare of his blazing digital clock, which shouted out my sleepless minutes.

Beneath his beatific face, I could see tsunamis, cyclones, and zombies arise; he'd whimper and fight big psychic battles in which I had to intervene before he killed me. Oh, it was a rodeo some nights, as I'd roll him bucking onto his side and pin down his legs, pull his feet into a pillowcase, and tie them off with a couple of sleep masks. Then we'd be in dreamland at last until he sought his cell phone ringing somewhere inside my blankets and body cavities. I'd get up early, so he got hours to abuse the pillows on his own, most of which ended up on the floor, yards from the bed.

We deployed herbs, medications, meditations, and it was getting better all the time. Now that I was making him meals, slipping him grains in lieu of glutens, goat dairy in place of cow, his labored breathing eased. And his Hannibal Lecter machine went into storage.

I had to stop and evaluate. I was good for him and for me, and there were many compensations for the sleep wars. He'd tuck me in each night with a bonus back rub and a paternal peck on the top of my head, and I'd sleep double deep till his shift started. Then, if he knocked himself out sufficiently, the smell of his head was my sedative, his body the womb from which I wish I'd been born. I adored him and was proud to be with him. And he would cheer my performances and brag about my talents to his friends and family, who were becoming mine.

I was pleased to share with friends that, even unconscious,

he was very talented. His animal impersonations—trumpeting elephants, growling tigers, hidden kittens—were unbeatable. He could honk like a donkey or a flock of geese; whistle for a New York cab with one nostril stuffed. His coughs could open in *La Bohème* at the Met.

I loved to touch his sleeping hand and have it clamp onto mine like a Venus flytrap, till it was nearly gangrenous from the pressure. I loved the way he'd reach for me each morning, making out with a pillow till he finally located me among the covers.

After a year of sleeping most nights together, I awoke amazed at the creature comfort subsuming our lives. My free-floating anxiety was sinking in his ocean of devotion. Nothing had ever warmed my feet like his, my hands like his, my heart like his. Clearly ours was a love that made it worth losing sleep.

LOVE BATH

This is very bad. As soon as we got up to the assisted living's VIP guestroom, he said nothing. Just ran me a hot bath, poured in a little bottle of bath gel, ushered me quickly into the bubbles, put on the overhead heater, slammed the door, and left me to stew in my own juices.

How I hate that sweet Stan saw me lose it with my mother tonight.

Up since 6:00 a.m., we'd been imprisoned in abusive airport and airplane seats from LAX to Newark. Then we'd driven three hours to New Haven on ice in an Avis reeking of other people's Parmesan or worse, with a fake lavender disinfectant failing to obscure it. My neck was kinked in dimensions I've never known from the stress of arriving three hours late, prolonging this pilgrimage to share the news of our big decision to live together with my mother. His idea.

At 9:00 p.m. EST, I'd knocked hard on the door of her apartment at the assisted living facility, just in case she didn't have her hearing aids in or on. Yanking it open like she'd been lurking there, she hissed, "Shh! People are sleeping! It's about time you got here." She looked me over. "You couldn't comb your hair, wear lipstick? What if somebody sees you!"

I strained a smile, hitting my consonants hard. "It's absolutely terrific to see you, too, Mother. May we come in?"

She felt the gibe. Her nostrils flared, my upper arms clenched to my sides. Tension gelled between us . . . until she saw Stan.

"Hello again, Fran," my featured creature crooned with his warmest, most placating face. She melted into his arms with a sigh. "Calm down," he mouthed to me over her shoulder. He's the perfect palliative, the lamb I will now sacrifice on the pyre of my mother.

Ow. My back is spasming in this ergonomically terrible tub. The water makes my body look puffy, misshapen—in this awful light I'm yellowed and withered, freckled and veiny. I feel self-conscious in front of myself, wearing nothing but a shower cap and glasses. And I've got this blister on my forehead from burning myself with the curling iron early this morning. Feel like I've been in a fight. Good there's a bathroom door and wall between me and him right now.

My mother is silly putty in his hands. What woman would not tenderize in those eyes? I practically lactate when he smiles. But feeling good about him is making me feel creepier about myself right now. I am regressing into a self-assassinating, pre-therapy incubus. I'm reviewing every frame of the scene as he might have seen it. I force myself strenuously to see this from my own perspective.

We'd stepped inside her tidied doll's house of an apartment, leaving our bags in the hall. All the units here were similar to our VIP guest room upstairs, hers the smaller one-bedroom style with kitchenette. Since she'd shrunk about three inches and too many pounds, she bought small. All her furniture seemed diminutive, like little girl things. She was teenier than last time; her sweater dwarfed her. She's melting like the Wicked Witch of the

West—my witch. I might lose her any minute. I leaped over the gulf to hug her—with true caring. She was resistant. I clung on. She didn't like me right now. So I wouldn't like her back. Her silver-haired do was glass-wool stiff; its chem trail up my nostrils made them burn. She patted me off on the back a few times, dismissing me with "too tight," and reached to hug him far longer, as he rocked her side to side to side. She likes him best.

"I wish I still had a mother to hug," he said.

I wish I for once had a mother I could rock side to side.

A wave of self-pity washes over me, and I run more hot water to comfort myself. I'm too aware of the rust stains around the faucet, how this awful fluorescent overhead in this institutional white-tiled bathroom makes me feel like I'm being cross-examined by myself. The rattling motor of the overhead heater is further torture.

What's going on in the adjoining guest bedroom? Is he reconsidering? Living with me may not look so appealing now. Boy, would it be *infuriating* if he changed his mind now, after I'd made so much damn space in my house for him, thrown so much away.

When his sneakers crept into my closet, I gladly dumped three killer pairs of spike heels and some ill-conceived blue platform boots I never even liked. Then he started getting into my other drawers—even the bottom ones reserved for bottoms. Okay. His bottoms deserved not to be piled on the floor anymore, and, as I could wear his shorts, too, I consolidated. I sorted my onesie camisoles from the bikinis; the little-boy undies that bunch in the crotch from the waist-high ones I'd saved for waist-high pants I'd be throwing out, too; the what-was-I-thinking thongs from the Wonder Butts, and folded his two pair of plaid shorts into their place.

The lingerie was hard to let go, but overdue. I opened that dank top bureau drawer just last week, and a compressed projectile of dressy boned longlines; booster pads of assorted sizes; tangled elastic stretch straps for convertibles, strapless, halter-style, and racer backs; removable silicone gel chicken cutlets; cutting-edge underwired; front loaders; back hookers; jogger bra pullovers; hydraulic push-ups; and workout tops with perky built-ins exploded in my face.

I slashed apart a Gordian knot of mementos, feeling like a paleontologist finding fossils of myself—nipple itchers, hydraulic pusher uppers, WonderBras. I recalled the men I'd worn them for, how anticipating their approval turned me on to myself, how cruelly I used to compress tender parts of my viscera in hopes of a hot time. Did I ever really wear that one with holes the nipples would stick through, the other that placed a perfect fleur-de-lis across the areola? Bye bye. I only have two breasts, wear one bra a day if at all, and if things go well may soon have a live-in male who could care less about lace, whose favorite style of underwear is off. I would trade all the trappings of my oversexed middle-age for the stability of monogamy now.

My mother has met him twice before. They'd talked endlessly about her life last time. They're intimates now. Clearly, she likes him better than me, as do I right now. Beyond his wash-and-wear hair and moist, multilobed mouth that never needs lip balm, he's a shrink with three plus decades of experience. He'd be a built-in counselor. Nah. He probably wouldn't want to come home to a nutcase with a moody mother who longs to reveal our troubled underside, the whole *Hellzapoppin'* farce of our family. But luckily, he gets her, and she considers him her colleague. I hope he doesn't buy into the little revenges she'll seek since I took a tone with her.

I try to do my stupid double-vision thing, trying to see how appealing I might look to him at my current worst, then imagining the whole scenario as a hybrid from his and Mom's eyes, obliterating my hard-won self-acceptance. *Get a grip.*

"May we please sit down?" I'd smiled too muscularly at my grouchy mother.

"Go ahead." She gestured to two undersize rockers with tufted pillows in her parlor, decorated with tchotchkes my NY set designer sister chose for her, and we squeezed ourselves in and rocked. Norma's presence was palpable as she and her husband drove dutifully in from Brooklyn to visit our mother often, as I from LA could not.

Lowering herself into her recliner with a theatrical moan of exhaustion, she tilted herself slowly back to hold court. She's still cute. I'm glad, as her appearance may be a map of mine.

"Aren't you tired? It's after nine already," she yawns noisily.

"We're wired. We're on California time," he soothes.

"Well, I'm on old lady time, and for me it's very, very late."

"Do you want us to leave right now, Mom?" I hoped her hearing aids would filter the snippiness out of my voice, but my strained lilt penetrated. She rolled me her whites-of-the-eyes look, gritted her teeth. Oh, yes, she will retaliate, warn him about me. Her recall can get very specific about my past sins. These last couple years, I'd told him some of my backstory in honest generalities—not to withhold, but because between us we had 123 years, all thick with colorful histories to share. We shared only what seemed germane in the moment. Now, after that awkward scene, seeing this nasty side of me, he might think our last two years together were all a charade, in which he perceived me as, and I played the role of, sweetness itself—a construct of our infatuation. Was it? Was I? I speed search my soul.

No! I just get happier as we get closer, and rule in favor of my-self. I love the way we laugh, the way we work things out. How we simply get polite with each other when we're miffed. That's as bad as it gets so far. Different from the bellowing my father did when I quarreled with him at the age of eight.

He clutched his heart, exaggerating angina. "You are the *Bad Seed*!" he whimpered as nod to his favorite movie—in which Patty McCormack played an eight-year-old psychopath—and he popped one of his nitroglycerin pills. He truly imagined himself my victim, attributing to me killer traits if I said I wouldn't finish supper. How formative these favorite family films had been in creating my self-image. "You're trying to give me a heart attack!" he'd cry. "You'll be the death of me!"

Right—I am the demon daughter. No wonder I became an actor, an intensity addict so young. His rages were Learian in stature, my mother's Ophelian in helplessness.

I'm anxious, getting morbid and maudlin, escalating. *STOP*.

Thank goodness for meditation forays, which help me halt, rise above, and witness my madness, to survey my compulsive topic-jumping growing rampant. *Breathe*.

Think positive—like the wonderful workers at this senior center who welcomed us tonight. They must be in some kind of cult—cheery no matter how unpleasant the elders or the aromas, no matter how late the hour. Their unconditionally accepting em-brace of it all makes me feel spiritually stingy. But they have no ancient history with my mother, aren't triggered by her barbs. I'm sure she never bares her teeth with them. She needs them too badly, milks that sweet old-lady thing. If you baby her, she loves you; blow through her nice lady mythology, she'll kill you.

Steady. I must review my blessings. I still have all my own teeth, my own hair, my own breasts, my original mother. Few of my friends do; one no longer has her own life—people you love can go irreversibly away. *STOP.* Turn the tide. Positives? My man will soon move his sweet sentimentality into my home, the pictures of his kids, his three big brothers and their loving, gifted families, his late mother and father—the legendary saints. All will be hanging in my office. I'll be grateful for the crowd, as I have only my mother and sister as blood ties on earth. I have too little baggage for this stage of life. Sweet sixty-four and never been married, and starting all over again, for the, oh, maybe seventh time, but only the third time in my life I've lived with a man and would be saying those hackneyed syllables "I love you," without an "I do." We'd be shacking up, co-habiting, sharing expenses.

His two-toned silver hair makes me look younger in our photos, even though I'm five years older. I got so lucky. With him I'm goofy and awkward, a kid renewed. I play with the suds in the tub, put bubbles on my breasts, my chin, my shower cap.

I recall my mother's parting shot as we left her to go to our room tonight.

"So? Aren't you a little old to keep dying your hair?"

If my man was ignoring the illusion of my anachronistic auburn tresses before, it was right in his face now. I spun in the hallway and yelled loud like could wake the dead if they had their hearing aids in: "*IS IT YOUR GOAL TO COMPLETELY HUMILIATE ME!?*"

I could not help it. She clenched her teeth at me, "SSHHHH!!"

Now it was a victim standoff between her and me as we glared at each other—like in *High Noon*, one of those old cowboy movies

Dad loved—like we're in a showdown between underdog slingers fighting for the bottom, for who got hurt worse by the other

STOP. Breathe. Cut her some slack. She's nearly ninety. Try to see all her little criticisms as Jewish motherly advice. I imagine there are rules for offspring posted at this midrange assisted living campus in which my sister and I enrolled her with our dead dad's money:

1. *All daughters must wear lipstick, and smile incessantly when visiting their mothers, no matter how their mothers provoke them, how their fight-or-flight secretions unsettle them.*

2. *All mothers may criticize their daughters' hairstyles and bodies in front of their boyfriends. Feeling humiliated is your personal option.*

3. *No bitching back at mothers over eighty because if she drops dead during the night, it'll be all your fault and you'll never get over it.*

According to her tonight, I'd willfully head-butted my way out of her poor little body at birth, my skull so big the doctor thought I was wearing a helmet. She had to get stitches. Even as a fetus I was ill-intentioned. Stan just nodded and absorbed as he rocked.

"And the whole area still hurts me," she says.

Way too much information. I do not want my boyfriend imagining my mother's areas. I can't blame dementia for her lack of filter. She's sharp as a tack, her thinking very clear. She remembers way too many things from fifty years ago, and too vividly. She was taking life in such baby steps she couldn't see beyond our household, while I was dreaming of Parisian adventures at age ten. She knows exactly what she's doing—trying to convince my boyfriend, super empath that he is, how helpless she is, was, how imperfect and selfish I am, will always be. If I dare tell her our moving-in together news, she'll talk him into moving in with her instead.

Damn. I had a stupid romantic fantasy of how this would go tonight. I'd tell her teary-eyed, tender like a young maiden, that this featured creature is my "one." How we had gone through all the right falling-in-love steps for our age group:

First base: Kissing, just like the old days, short and long, but with far more meaningful eye contact and genuine affection balancing the lust.

Second base: Sharing the same bed, despite our insomnia-phobe sensitivities; really deep sleeping in both long dreams and short subjects and reaching for a leg touch often to make sure we're still there.

Third base: Necking. Kissing, licking, and sucking one another's throats and around the ears. I loved that, and so did he—for one night. Used to keep a couple occupied for weeks. I can't remember when I last necked. It must be out of style. I haven't seen a hickey since high school.

Fourth base: Petting above the waist. Fondling torsos actually kept us happy when we were young, before contraceptives made below the waist okay. The new generation skips this entirely, going right for blow job. We went for long, soulful conversations between regions.

Fifth base: Finally going all the way, after lingering in preliminaries for months. Despite time blurring by so fast, we were both anxious about rushing into attachment at the speed of youth. We both had wounds to protect, and despite decades of healing, they were raw. And, of course, we had to navigate the mysteries of my migrating orgasm (is it here? or over there?), the timing of his erection; to preplan positions that favored our prior injuries. It was working great.

Fifth base: Spending Friday nights through Monday mornings together and truly bonding, cooking, showering.

Sixth base: Meeting his family and kids, and him meeting Mom last year.

The bases are so overloaded with our love, I planned to say, that he must now move into my house for easier access. I'd fantasized she might happily snap into my dream mom. She'd hold me to her bosom, wherever the hell that's even located now, and caress my hair and my back without patting me off.

Her mood made me want to hoard our news from her. She'd make it dirty anyway. "Why buy the cow if you can get the milk for free," or some such obscenity to ruin things, to make them ugly in her envy. That meant if a man had had sex with you and lived with you first, why would he bother to marry you? I'd prewritten retorts so I wouldn't cave in to insecurities of my own.

"This cow can't be bought, Mother. It owns its own damn pasture, and it's gotten so much men's milk for free, it's lactose intolerant."

Although this cow always did secretly dream it would be legally married, a legitimate next of kin, cherished, honored, and obeyed. Although a fierce feminist, it's still a romantic, an old-fashioned one, and it's been growing a great love in a big, tender heart saved for a forever friend all its long life.

Thinking pragmatically, on the other hand—it was probably best for it to stay a girlfriend, independent, with its own last name, without all the legal-schmegal trappings and entanglements of nuptials. I'd eluded all those messy complications this long. Marriage was a trap for women. Look what happened to my mother and her mother, and all the downtrodden, demeaned damsel wives of yore.

In the role of greatest girlfriend ever, I have always excelled. There for my men through thick and thin, without needing to be paid in jewelry—I'm not a jewelry type. Hey, I never needed nuptials to care and be there for my friends. What a ghastly word, *nuptials.* C'mon. Wife, husband, wedding band, trousseau—so throwback, barbaric, so ownership-oriented. As long as Stan and I are together, I'll be good.

He might be changing his mind after seeing me snap at my little old mother. Damn. I'd so hoped we'd all have a fun time. But she was already pissed by the time we got there, as if we had planned to strand her at supper, where she'd hoped to show us off.

STOP. Feel the deeper layer. Here I am, two floors away from my only mother, with the man I love most in the next room, and I'm feeling that ol' familiar alienation and aloneness in the world. I examine the handicapped rail on the wall next to the tub— seniors need those for balance, as tubs are places of treachery. That's a harbinger of what's ahead for me—the unpredictability of aging, the constant improvisation of adaptations, the letting go of faculties, the—

He taps at the bathroom door. "Hello? Can I come in?"

I reflexively cover my breasts, feeling shy, shivery.

"Sure."

He enters in those cute plaid undershorts, puts his wrist in the bath like a daddy would, leans over, turns on the hot faucet to raise the temperature and level of water, and adds more bath gel.

"Room for me in there?" He looks deep into my eyes for the right kind of permission.

"Yes," I say, sitting up, raising my knees to make space. He drops his drawers, adorable, while I feel unattractive, my own skin a stranger. So many moles, you could play connect the dots on me. He turns off the water, eases his immaculate skin in, avoiding the awful spout. (Why can't they put the damn faucets and spouts on the side wall?) He sighs and slides down to face me. We fit ourselves in as the drain slurps and belches commentary, and the overhead heater's timer dings off, and without the red hue, even he looks tired. And then it's quiet except for our sloshing. We're tense. He reaches for my foot. I surrender it, more reserved about my toes than I feel about exposing my still legitimately brown-haired possum. My feet are shy. I'm usually not a fan of feet, but his are kind of like low maintenance pets I don't have to feed, walk, or curb. I cuddle them amicably along my sides like puppies.

Mmm. He rubs me nice like he still likes me. I grin; he smiles. Clearly, this man graduated from the Baby Panda Bear School of Cute—his gaze the most satisfying I'd ever allowed almost all the way inside me. How must I look to him? He seems to really like me and think I'm cute. I think he's cute, too. Even when we're mad, or our hair's stringy, or we're sick, or we make mistakes, we still like each other. After two years of getting closer and closer, I still think looking prettier might give me more leverage in love. That my deficits are overlooked if I have a lucky-looking day. I would never know until I let myself go if that were true, and I wasn't about to start now, vain bitch that I might always be.

"Your mother's a challenge," he says.

"Sorry I yelled back like that," I put a bouquet of suds on his knee as peace offering.

"You two really push each other's buttons," he massages my other foot. He recognizes I'm not completely at fault.

Relieved, I feel like a cowering, mangy cur, forgiven for peeing in the house. He's kind. And for this aspect I have accepted his absent-mindedness and his messiness, forgiven his unkempt car. I can learn to live with that. Are there any other annoying things I should note before he gives up his apartment to commit to my home and me full-time forever because we're too old and tender to go through retreating from each other?

I do envy his ability to eat anything that has ever lived, in a fermented, pickled, smoked, marinated, brined, or corned past, while my delicate system can only ingest filtered air on alternate Tuesdays with a side of sterilized water. Living without love for so long damaged my constitution. Maybe his love, if applied consistently over time, will let me bite into more of life. He compensates by being very generous. He splurged at a new place last week where we were served orbs impersonating eyeballs that dissolved on contact with our mouths into deconstructed olives, and a green meringue volcanic mountain that erupted into a small stain of watercress sauce beneath a monkfish. A gelled carrot soup square, served on a bed of popcorn air, was more of an idea of food than actual food. Much a-goo about nothing, but it was fun to appreciate the artistry, then devour the contents in two bites.

Lately there's his penchant for cooking. This last month, he's offered to make me Sunday dinners in my kitchen. Now on Saturdays he becomes a hunter-gatherer, roaming far, wide, and wild to capture something truly throwback to cook. He has an especially soft spot for entrails—things that would have simply been read by seers in the Middle Ages, then fed to wild dogs, most not allowed by the board of health past the disposal cans of the slaughterhouse or the rabbi. I tolerated the goat kidneys in garlic, beef hearts in bacon, oxtails in leeks, chopped chicken livers and onions in schmaltz because he shares my late father's poor-man food values: throw nothing away, and take all day to make it. But this Mr. Delicious believes in using every surface of the kitchen and every tool I have. He cooks like he dances—a whirling, reckless dervish.

Far be it from me to discourage him from taking charge of felling, skinning, boning, and flaming a meal for me. But when he ripened tripe in tomato sauce for hours last weekend, stewing offal, melting Stilton, I lost my appetite. He dined alone, and I sealed myself off behind doors, air filters, and masks, put police tape around the kitchen. He cleaned up, fortunately.

C'mon, admit it. I want him. His understanding nature outweighs these idiosyncrasies. These small irritations, far from irreparable conflicts, might make good material someday.

I grow aware of his tension, that he is far more unsettled than miffed at me. I'm about to ask what's on his mind when suddenly, out of nowhere, lifting two hands of my dripping, water-raisined fingers in his, like some man in a movie, he says,

"Will you marry me?"

I freeze. A complete non sequitur. Is he doing a bit? That would be really mean. Doesn't he know how upset I am about my mother's judgments and my intolerance? About how badly I want to be married to him? I prepare to be hurt, gird my pale, dimpling loins.

STOP. Before overreacting and acidifying, premeditate. Don't intuit ill intent. Slow down the knee-jerk speed of volatility right now. Get in the moment. Look.

His question has red-rimmed his big blue eyes; his voice is vulnerable as though he's moved himself in asking, like something big's at stake. I've had little sleep—I could be dreaming, or night-maring. But I'm too aware of the elastic of the too-tight shower cap cutting into my forehead, my glasses sliding down my nose, the burn on my forehead. I must be awake.

If he was sincere, could he have rigged a camera in the toilet tank? I've watched so many YouTube proposals lately featuring elaborately staged musical numbers with casts of friends danc-ing around an unsettled bride-to-be; seen people propose on Jumbotrons in stadiums, and in movie theaters, a scream erupt-ing from the unsuspecting maiden in the audience as she watches a trailer featuring her boyfriend proposing to her in 3-D. I try to imagine myself blushing, flustered as a swirl of rehearsed se-nior citizens and staff poured into this assisted living bathroom to sing to me. It could be my most spontaneous filmed moment ever.

Nah. There'd have been no way to set that up. A spike of in-dignation that he hadn't orchestrated an elaborate musical pro-duction; hadn't rehearsed it for weeks; that we were in the most unromantic of locations; that I was my most unphotogenic ever; that he was wasting a momentous event that might have made good drama pierced me.

I'm in the actor's nightmare. In a film or play, not knowing my lines or moves, forgetting my motivations as the man playing opposite me drops to one knee, and his amplified voice booms across a concert hall for all the world to see, the unexpected mag-ical question hovering in the air.

"Will you marry me?"

What's my line?

No one I could ever take seriously has ever asked me this simple question in real life before. I'd imagined being asked by loves I'd lost many times in the most romantic of locations and circumstances and wondered how I'd react if I were ever really on the spot. In most cases, negatively, which always clarified why, despite the interminable heartaches, those loves were best left lost. And I'd been asked and said yes in plays, musicals, and television shows, in which I'd been married many times and had many kids, endured many courtships and childbirths.

Onstage and in films, I'd walked down four aisles and run headlong down another. Some ceremonies had sound and lighting men crawling under my feet, and hundreds of extras. My actual family was never invited. Three of my husbands died—two in comedies, one in a drama. I didn't mourn long, but it sobered me just imagining how much anguish is suffered when one loses one's true love.

On one funny series, a handsome plastic surgeon performed an emergency nose job on my character when she fell face first. He proposed to the results of his nose artistry as soon as she healed. After he keeled over dead during our ceremony, the writers wrote me a rebound wedding to another man . . . who died on our honeymoon in Hawaii.

Out of pity for me, the show's costume designer slipped this still single middle-aged spinster one of the beautiful wedding gowns to keep—gorgeous, cut to fit me. I thanked him fervently.

"Bill, I'm going to wear this gown someday for real."

"Of *course* you are, dear," he murmured, patting my old-maid hand.

I had kept that gown wrapped in plastic in my closet like Miss Havisham in *Great Expectations* for twenty-five years now. I would take it out to look at it every few years and renew my vow to wear it. I'd save a thousand dollars on a new one if I did. Would

I finally get to take her out and put her on for real?

I rehearsed all the feelings of love in so many stories for so many years, I wondered if that show would ever open. Long had I longed for a commitment for life, rather than a flimsy contract for run-of-show, long had I pined for a real ceremony after which no one yelled, "Cut!"

And now my first non-actor had asked me.

Could this really be happening here and now? How could anybody ask to marry a woman wearing nothing but glasses and a shower cap in a bathtub at an old-age home. He must be crazy. Or could it be he really loves me?

Oh, I know better than anything I ever knew to be true that I really love him—I'm afraid of how much I love him. I can tell by my actions toward him. I can tell by my acceptance of him. I can tell by the way he makes me laugh, by the way I melt at his public adoration of me, who has always watched love like it was a spectator sport. I can tell he's been falling deeper for me, as lately he's stopped stepping over the newspaper as he leaves for his office in the morning and started bringing it all the way into the house, sometimes onto my bed—even my belly. He's now washing the greasy undersides of the dishes and pots, instead of just swiping around the tops. Like moss on the north side of a tree, these are Nature's signs of a man's devotion.

I begin to plot. If this is real, if I said, "Yes, please!" he might go down on one knee and ask my mother to be his mother-in-law, which is maybe why he talked me into this trip. This might prolong and uplift my mother's life a little, give her more respect for me. It might give others and me more respect for me, too. I can go from transient gypsy who goes from job to job, show to show, charity event to charity event, man to man, to a permanent role. From freelance fringe outcast, ever the odd woman out, to a member of a real, functional family. I might go from exiled artist to trophy stepmom to his incredible kids, whom I've held myself back from loving. I can leap into another dimension of living, of being. I can feel what forever feels like gazing at his ever-changing face, into his big-sky eyes. I can have the grace of growing old loved after decades of isolation.

Wait. I'd better make sure this incongruent incident was not hallucinated, and, if actual, that it wasn't just his momentary whim. I hold my breath for a moment.

"Well?" He's tensing for a no.

"*What?*" I squeak. "*Reeeaally?*" I'm quaking.

"Yes." He sees how it's going to go.

"I thought I'd have to be perfect first. I won't ever be perfect."

"Me, neither."

"I can't ever be an apron-wearing, wifey-type wife."

"I know that."

"Cheery, smiling all the time . . . I get mad . . ."

"You're real." He pushes my glasses back up my nose.

"I was confused and made a lot of misery in my life, for me and other people."

"Me, too." He sits back from his supplicating posture. "That's why we get each other so well. All that grief and guilt and low self-esteem about it." He actually understands.

"Everybody's been so suspicious of why I haven't married. Especially me."

He takes calm command, like he's instructing a small plane pilot on how to land in a storm from the control tower. "Hey, I did it once in my twenties and failed, and lots of my tries tanked after that. You and I both want it enough to keep trying. We wouldn't be ready now if we hadn't blown it before."

Hedges were still lining up in my head, like planes circling JFK.

"What would your kids say? They already have a mother."

"Before I met you, you were already their favorite mother from that cartoon series."

I was grateful for the advantage acting gave me in this situation.

"And while you were in the bath, I called and told them I was going to ask you, and they said, 'It's about time.'" He takes my hands out of the water again and, with his from-the-heart thing, murmurs, "I want you to be part of my family."

My face contorts—I've never been a pretty weeper—but I forgive myself—I'm moved.

"Listen." His voice is somber. "We both have to take the risk to trust each other and trust ourselves to love each other fully."

I muster one last warning: "You know, I might look like this more often as I age," then, "I suppose you'll never look this good, either."

"Age is going to have its way with us—who knows how it will go down," he says. "And by the way, to me, you've never looked more beautiful."

I try to do my stupid double-vision thing, trying to see how appealing I might look to him at my current worst. But before that blurry headache comes on, I give myself the gift of mercy, the grace of letting inhibitions go. Now that he wants to tie the knot, I'm aware that another big chunk of residual mistrust is slipping away. Wasn't even aware of it till now. Sure, he's semi-moved in, I've made space in my home and my psyche. But now that he popped the question and we'll have a real ceremony and the whole shebang in front of witnesses, all reserve is vaporizing. How shallow I am to need all those silly, superficial, old-fashioned things so much to surrender. But I *do*, dammit. I *do*! How very ironic that I might get married at the same age that my mother finally got divorced. The symmetry that my unconscious maybe had in mind strikes me as hilarious.

I notice he looks even more gorgeous loving me in this unobstructed forever sort of way. This may be the only man I can and will ever fit. And trusting him makes it safe to love him back so much bigger than I have ever loved anyone or anything before.

"Then, *yes!*" I cry. And I hear the complexity in my own voice saying yes.

I have said yes a million times in my life—yes, I like you; yes, I'll have more chicken; yes, I'll stay over—but I have never heard myself say yes like this before. So many layers in one little syllable—relief, grief, fear, desperation, determination. He hears them all, accepts them all.

I dove and noticed something inside me was there to catch me beyond him—a me who felt more credible and solid, more unified and dependable. Yes. I would be good for him and let him be good for me. I would take the risk to speak and do, without hiding to sort myself out. No rehearsal. No blur between selves, no headache practicing how to behave, trying to see from the outside how I looked or hear what I said before I took the risk to speak. This is how I look. This is how I sound. This is no longer a role in a play or a fiction. I am a real woman. And now I will belong, in a real shared life.

"I love you!" comes out of my mouth for the thousandth time in my life, but with an extra special intonation to the best man for me ever.

I throw myself on him for a rubbery, awkward hug. And we dry each other off with scratchy institutional towels and fall into the bed. He falls easily into sleep, smiling. I wake up in wonderment every few minutes all night, feeling the tides of my mind turning, the cells in my body reorganizing.

"Oooh," I say, touching his face with an unfettered, "we are *engaged!*"

And when he awakes the next morning and opens his eyes to mine, I feel happy that my mother won't hurt me so much anymore. After all, she will not be strolling into the sunset with me. He will be my family now. And I will never go on another date. I am a fucking *fiancée*. I will be his w-w-w-wife. Hah! This very unfamiliar word makes my lips itch, even just saying it silently to myself.

By morning my back is magically unkinked. My horror about that dreaded question Mom would have asked—"Why live together, why not get married?"—a question I myself had buried deep and undetected in my shitload of shame and unworthiness, has drained away.

I bask in unfamiliar sensations of security and contentment, relaxed in an absence of ache.

Odd. Woman. Out. In. Love. At last—and it was such a long damn time coming.

LOVE AT FIRST SEDER

I remember the attraction that day was instant and made me very anxious.

Her father's courtship of me had only been in progress a few months when he invited me to a Seder that she and other relatives would attend. I knew from experience that it was too soon, as an attachment could form with folks I might not see again.

Unmarried all my life, I'd had many, many starter relationships. Children I'd known for only a few holidays had left my sad lap as I disconnected from the guy who put them in it. But my new friend and I already felt familial, so I took a big chance.

As we entered his favorite aunt Sandy's home, there was his daughter, Ariana—sweet-faced like her father, big blue eyes, wise for her years. She hugged me firmly, fully to her heart. I was instantly girl-crush smitten. She introduced me to her fiancé, Marc, as my promising Passover escort left us to talk on our own.

Marc was Ariana's first love. He'd recently asked her father for her hand in marriage, then put a big fat diamond on it. I'd never had one and, awed at the many facets of her and hers, wondered what it was like to be betrothed and so secure in love at just twenty-three years old. I'd not yet known that kind of certainty and comfort in my life.

These two had their heads firmly on their shoulders, unlike

other young heads I'd known that tended to roll right off. She was getting her master's in social work, and he was earning his in engineering. They were smart, cultured, and, like me, musical theater lovers. She could sing in sweet soprano every lyric to every score of every contemporary musical. I'd sing back lyrics of musicals I'd learned in my musical heyday, in my twenties and thirties. Marc hummed along on them all. We three had so much to harmonize about that her father receded in my attentions just a little.

The rest of my date's family was more reserved. Apparently, I was not the first nice Jewish date her father had brought to Passover. His family was very observant. If I married into this group, I'd have to convert to a little bit more Jewish than I currently presented. Fortunately, I'd played many roles on the Jewish spectrum in my career, with varying shades of accents, so was undaunted. They seated me across from Ariana, next to her father. As we noshed on parsley, his uncle gave me a small portion of the Haggadah to read, and it felt like a tryout. I was bold in rewording it to include the female perspective. Ariana liked that, and I liked that she liked it. Well-versed in gender politics, she whispered of her wish to work with cisgender and transgender clients alike. Her knowledge of all the pronouns and proclivities amazed me. My focus on the bitter herbs faded, as I took stock of some blessings.

Why is this Seder different from all other Seders? I thought. Because this time I had a big crush on my date's daughter. My delight with her was now straining neck and neck with my held-in-check delight with her dad. I began thinking way too far ahead. She certainly didn't need my mothering. Her bio parents had done a fine job with all the heavy lifting, the bearing, the rearing, the weaning. Ariana was independent, loving, smart, and as tall as I was; pulling her into my lap would be unwieldy. Already in the midst of her blissful engagement, she wouldn't need my relationship counseling, my long dating life littered with frogs and other plagues.

"What could I offer her beyond old showtunes?" was one of the Four Questions I asked myself that night.

We harmonized a hearty "Go Down Moses," and as we parted, I felt a pang. I so hoped to see her again but would have to hold myself in check and hope her dad and I grew closer over time. Maybe if I played my cards right, I could get them all.

I soon fell for his younger son, Sam, too, a manly nineteen, and a groovy, get-down dancer at every event I attended. I was a fan. I got included in all the next big moments in Ariana's life—her graduation, her receiving of awards, her next Passover, at which everyone now knew my name and gave me more Haggadah portions to read and more portions to eat. I was passing all the Passover tests.

It would have been enough, I thought, to meet this wonderful man, but I got to dance with Sam and sing at Ariana's wedding to Marc a year later. "Dayenu".

And when her father asked me to marry him, I asked him if his daughter would feel okay about it.

"Are you kidding?" he said. "After the first Passover, she asked, 'Please, Daddy? Can we keep this one?' And I said yes—maybe for a long time."

So as a seasoned bride, not only did Ariana help me plan our wedding, at the reception she harmonized with me to some of my favorite old showtunes that she'd learned by heart.

OFF-ROADING

My brain slaps me upside the head when I travel. "Alert all offline systems," it says. "Open lazy lizard inner eyelids, which doze through ordinary days, and get ready for everything new, new, new. Metabolic processes, accelerate. Mouth, glut with words to explain all you see to anyone who will listen."

I like me so much more on the road. Curiosity shuts down my cowardice; distaste for discomfort fades as I leave the land of errands and brand names, the same old foods and rooms. I stop my frenetic dance away from the horrors of the mundane. I back-burner monotony, my fears of meaninglessness. I see the world and me from a different vantage point from inside my better-late-than-never, sixty-five-year-old, first-time-bride life.

"Are you bringing toothpaste?" handsome asks, throwing things together last minute, while I've voted on each of my items for weeks.

"Yes." I remove the redundant jumbo tube from his pile.

I see him differently, too, when we travel. Having arranged our trip—airlines, hotels, dinners—he feels heroic. This will lead to medicinally assisted hot hotel sex as we break in foreign beds like dangerous strangers strewing clothes around the unfamiliar room. I look forward to waking up not knowing where we are, who he is, who I am, what the hell happened to my underpants, and where the hell's the bathroom.

I'll thrill at his manhandling of my luggage, his computing of exchange rates, his negotiating at markets, his chatting up the cabbies, his tact with the tour guides. He gets teenaged. He doubles my exaltation at monuments that dwarf us, natural wonders that exhilarate us, cuisines that amaze us, pantomimed conversations that tickle foreign hearts with baseline humors just like ours.

I snap out of my reverie. We've made it to the airport in ample time. We're passing through Lufthansa check-in pleased with our compact packing, our sleek wheeled luggage, our lightweight coats. And as he bends over to put a tag on his bag, I see it.

My face has a hot flash, forced into a new point of view. I've not seen him at this angle before, or at least lately. Maybe it's just an illusion born of gravity and the forelock at the crown of his head. I look more closely.

My husband has a bald spot.

For a moment, I think I'm looking at the wrong man, but no, that's the sweater I gave him for his birthday hugging his neck. I stare in shock. I feel the urge to cry out, to run away. I can't let on—it might shake his confidence. This must stay a secret between me and me. I'll take a deep breath, get grounded, look once again to verify.

A patch of pink at the top of his head, where a shock of two-tone gray explodes energetically out of his scalp, where it divides in all directions, running lustily for the sides of his head, is widening. Being inches shorter than he is, rarely higher up than he is, it's the first evidence of his aging I've registered. It looks shy, naked, new. I shrink, shake inside myself, and look away.

It's not the spot per se that makes me want to run and hide.

It's not that he's any less adorable. It's what it signifies. The map has changed. A gorge has emerged with this new life-size landmark. No Waze will show us any way around it, no rights or lefts or new roads. Google has not yet charted this locale.

I didn't factor in this development, that things that finally felt so fixed in my life could erupt in flux, that things that seemed under control inside the security of our sweetness could get so swiftly unsettled. This is how it starts. I tense up in resistance.

I've seen aging in myself, certainly. I've lost an inch in height. The skin of my thighs, which used to be taut, is not. My face, which used to be my calling card, is a falling card. Certain signs of decay no longer go away with a good night's sleep, acupuncture, exercise, or the care of my hairdresser. Certain evidence is irreversible. There's no way to stop the onset of puberty or the reminders of decay. We are growing older.

I've continued to cling to my image in my home bathroom mirror, in which I'm lit in a flattering way. I look okay for my age, I reassure myself. But in fluorescent-lit mirrors, in others' selfies, in car windows, or in the cruel distortions in my car's side mirror, I've caught a glimpse of myself and gotten disoriented. Who is this aging person? This crone in progress? This once confident woman who feels young and supple and surefooted and fast-witted looks a lot like my ninety-year-old mother.

With urgency I reconfigure how harsh my judgments can be, factoring in bad lighting, and reassure myself that no one sees me as skewed as I do. "You're too hard on yourself!" they would say, and I'd calm down. I stop by home periodically, not just for supplies, but to see myself in that one flattering mirror, to reassure myself that I still exist as I imagine myself. I smile to lift it all up, like for photo sessions, although I rarely look this way outside them. This delusion gives me the faith to face my days. In the hierarchy of biological needs, vanity vacillates between two and three.

I focus on the affections of my husband to confirm I'm not as bad as all that, knowing I'll have to face the truth one day, but please not yet. I'm not ready. No matter how much inner work I do, how much therapy I have, how much virtue I manifest from inside myself, vain and vapid bitch that I am, I may never be ready. I'll be ready for death before I'm ready to look other than I did in my heyday, when men said, "Hey."

Wait. Maybe he's already absorbed my many signs of erosion and is protecting me in the glow of his unconditional eyes, as I now plan to shield him in my white lies of love. But we always see the light in each other, so it's not really deceit. It's virtual surgery. It's a reconstructive visioning. We believe what we re-see. That's what love does.

He straightens up and smiles, gravity restored to his hair and head, and all returns to normal. And as we trudge along, I overly adore the back of him. I admire the socks I bought him as we de-shoe for the TSA. I enjoy my public pat down as he watches—it's erotic. It's probably the closest I'll ever get to lesbianism and he'll get to a three-way beyond buying lightbulbs.

Seated cozily in coach, I take hold of the hand that looks so sexy in that wedding ring with which I bound him to me, and we buckle each other in. Mmm. Bondage. I thrill at the miracle of flight from my window seat, in which I can watch the exact moment that the velocity of this monstrosity makes it lift off, when the wheels retract and we are by some miracle airborne and Peter Pan powerful.

Five hours in—wined, dined, and movied—we doze. I tuck

him in and pull a blanket over my eyes. At home, my husband and I sleep with a hut of pillows pulled over and around our faces. Ostensibly, it's to block out light and the sound of tweeting yard birds and phone alerts come dawn. But for me, it's also to hide my slackened countenance. I'm still bemused when he's revealed by an accident of tossing or turning, as he is now, openmouthed, sad eyed, snoring gently by my side.

I sneak an extended peek, and, without the animation of his huge presence, his face is funny, flaccid, his body like a marionette without a puppeteer, drooping on a hook, strings dangling, lifeless. But I give him a little kiss, and like magic he reanimates with a world-changing grin that wipes away decades and restores him to his habitual handsome. I'm not sure he's ever caught me in decomposing repose, or if he has, he's never let out a peep about it. I still get up first and toss my hair into a casual-seeming style, balm my lips, freshen my breath, and get back into the sanctuary of our Egyptian cotton habitat for morning cuddles.

This is the deal. Marrying in our sixties, we signed up for it all. We looked in each other's eyes, evaluated the ongoing attraction, the future, the dialogue, the humor, the extras, the liabilities, and so-the-fuck-whats, and knew this person was worth the risk.

Since we met late in life, the milestones that most married have hit decades earlier will be all squashed together into maybe two decades for us, tops. When we married, childfree me became an instant stepmom to his two incredible kids in their twenties. I met all my stepson's uniquely wonderful girlfriends. I went to college graduations in our first year and sang at my stepdaughter's wedding soon after. Now I stalk her womb like a madwoman, seeking signs of fecundity, hoping she might soon make me a step-grandmother. It's my latest biological need, which I've developed since we married, just when I thought all needs were satisfied. I got a bonus three brothers, two with wives and more amazing kids, and all their concomitant milestones fill our holidays with happy family events.

But all too soon, he and I will get old together, infirm together, and, if we are lucky, die together at the exact same second, which would save our heirs a lot of aggravation sorting through our stuff, the double dose of sorrow notwithstanding. We already have adjoining compartments for our ashes in an oaken box, in the hopes of simultaneous death, as compensation for our lack of simultaneous orgasms at this stage, as compensation for having waited for each other so damn long.

Or if fate plays it the hardest, most probable way for him and me, one of us will nurse and bury the other. One of us will grieve alone as the other abandons us and scorches the earth as s/he goes. One of us will be left keening, wrenched in half, relentlessly seeking comfort, when no comfort will exist outside the other's arms.

There was no choice for me but to love him, so there is no escape. I never dated a guy this old before, partly to avoid awareness of the inevitability of my own mortality, but also because I never found any older or younger ones this boyish and joyous. I fell all the way into love with this wonderful one for real. I remind myself that on a sane and sober day I found forever in this face. I knew I'd want to look at him every day, even when he pissed me off. Of all the men in the world, I have married only this one. I knew that the agonizing grief of losing each other would be worth it for the joy we'd have. I knew that as the loop of our lives was narrowed by age and the loss of our near and dears, sharing the center of it with him was the best fate I could imagine. I know that loving more double deep than we've ever loved will give us the courage to survive our lack of survival together.

We've landed in the Czech Republic and pull our blue bags from the merry-go-round filled with blank black ones, already excited by foreign accents saying excuse me. I love looking at their unfamiliar faces, the guilelessness of eyes that aren't from America. He bends over to get out his jacket, and I see it again. It is very real now. Embarrassed, I look away. I'd almost forgotten it amid our anticipation. I look again and linger, determined to get adjusted to it and what it means.

Funny how the aging trip, with its sudden departures into unknowns for which one only plans in generalities, with its new language, which only medical professionals will translate for us, with the adaptations that will be demanded of us as time flies by, is so much less welcome than the other surprises I so treasure when we journey to new places. Where the hell is my embrace of spontaneity, my openness to growth, to coping with the unknowns along the way?

Missing in action at this moment.

Could his hair maybe grow back and cover up the bald spot? Maybe it just dried funny and tomorrow it will be fine. Maybe he scratched at it like a cat at a flea, and this is temporary. Maybe there's a pill I can slip into his food to make it stop. I strenuously search for justification for denial. But wait. Could hair loss be happening to me, too? No. I have a fleet of intimate workers with whom I consult expensively, who can negotiate work-arounds on my hair, at least for a little while longer.

I wouldn't want him to work around. I loathe work-arounds on men—comb-overs, plugs like bristle brushes, toupees, dye jobs—though I admire the work-arounds on women and the artists who accomplish them. I have a big double standard there. I like my man au naturel, courageously facing the unknown, protecting me from my fears of the onslaught of aging. My husband is my brave explorer. I know he will carry this emblem with grace.

At that moment, I fall deeply in love with the bald spot atop him, and decide to adopt it. It's a whole new thing about him to cherish. It will be my new pet, a hidden motherless child I didn't know existed. It's young, vulnerable, innocent, and pink, like an infant's derriere. Dear little spot.

He straightens up, hoisting his bag, and offers one of his world-illuminating grins, surprised to see me gazing so tenderly at him, tears cresting in my eyes.

"What is it?" he asks.

"Nothing," I say. "I love you."

"I love you, too," he says. "Here we go!"

EPILOGUE

Love In The Time Of Coronavirus

For the first time in our five years of marriage,

my husband hears me fart.

As he lets his beard grow and I let my hair go,

other things get let go, too.

We've learned what we'll look like old and like it.

Working from home, nowhere to hide,

we laugh and weep more freely.

As sickness surrounds, our foreplay prolongs its joy

to drown out our sadness.

On our eighth of an acre, we are Adam and Eve in Eden,

picking onions, arugula, oranges,

eating al fresco in our yard. We've joined

the slow-food, slow-love, slow-life movement,

staying in the moment, taking it day by day by day. . .

PREVIOUSLY PUBLISHED

Sections of the following essays, published by these journals and magazines, appear in different forms and sometimes under different titles in *Odd Woman Out*. I own all rights.

Better After 50—"Many Weddings, Many Kids"

Bluestem Magazine—"The Undertow of Neptune"

Chicken Soup for the Soul: My Crazy Family—"Extra Helpings," published as "The Deli Fella"

Chicken Soup for the Soul: Age Is Just a Number—"Off-Roading" published as "Adventures in the Unknown"

Defenestration—"Car-isma"

Entropy—"The Trojan Horse," published as "Greeks Bearing Gifts"

Evening Street Review—"Happily Never After"

Five on the Fifth—"Sitting In"

Funny Times—"The Carcass"

Jewish Journal—"Deadly Bedding," published as "Sleeping Together"

Living the Second Act—"Letting Go of My Lingerie" and "My Many Pretend Marriages"

Purple Clover—"The Price of Popular," published as "My Secret Admirer"; "Frugging to Shakespeare," published as "The Go-Go Comeback"; and "Extra Crispy," published as "Wigging Out"

Verdad Magazine—"Off-Roading," published as "The Side Trip"

ACKNOWLEDGMENTS

First, I'm very grateful to my parents for all the great material. Then to Wendy Hammers, whose workshop prompts inspired several of the newer stories and whose "Tasty Words" productions gave several pieces their first public outings. Maggie Rowe put other newborn pieces into Comedy Central's Hollywood stage show "Sit n' Spin," as did Eve Brandstein, who included first versions in her "Poetry in Motion" performances. Grateful that Ronda Spinak midwifed some of my work in the Jewish Women's Theatre performances, and is rebirthing it on the *Chaiflicks* website.

Appreciate the wisdom of the Grapes boys, Jack the father who deepens the writer's voice, and Joshua the son, who thins out and rearranges the foliage so one can see the forest through the trees.

Many thanks to the Joshua Tree Comedy Festival, who commissioned and presented my musical memoir version of "Odd Woman Out" (songs available on request). I had never considered making a book out of it all until Charlotte Gusay saw me performing pieces around Los Angeles and insisted I consider it. Then the caring, constant, and constructively critical ears of Rima Goodman and Lyn Kupferman nurtured it as it grew.

Grateful, I'm part of the Tuesday night writers' group that

Barbara Bottner guides, and for the feedback I continue to receive from Arlene Schindler, Carol Schlanger, Roberto Loiderman, Susan Cuscuna, Stephanie Satie, and Kathleen Garrett there.

I am forever amazed by my late-to-the-party mate, muse, first, last and only h-h-husband (the word still makes my lips itch), my beloved Stan Friedman, whose love and wisdom makes life more meaningful and gives every story a happy ending.